THE COMPLETE GUIDE TO
BEDDING
PLANTS
FOR AMATEURS AND EXPERTS

THE COMPLETE GUIDE TO
BEDDING
PLANTS
FOR AMATEURS AND EXPERTS

Carolyn Jones

Voyageur Press

Edited by Elaine Jones
Cover photograph and interior photographs by David Jones
Cover and interior design by Bob English

Typeset at The Typeworks, Vancouver

Printed and bound in Canada by Friesen Printers, Altona, Manitoba

Library of Congress Cataloging-in-Publication Data

Jones, Carolyn, 1950–
   The complete guide to bedding plants for amateurs
and experts.

   (Pacific northwest gardening)
   Bibliography: p.
   Includes index.
   1. Bedding plants—Northwest, Pacific. I. Title
II. Series.
SB423.75 UJ 1989   635.9'62'09795   89-5534
   ISBN 0-89658-109-8

Contents

Preface

My first garden was a pie-shaped wedge of soil–if you could call it that–on our street corner in Chicago. When I was fifteen, I sprinkled a packet of marigold seeds over the surface, scratched them in a bit and watered. Every morning, I looked out of my bedroom window, waiting for the first sign of life. To my amazement, the seedlings grew and in a few months, I was the proud caretaker of a mass of orange flowers. One day when I was tending my little patch, an elderly woman stopped and spoke to me. She said she walked past my marigolds regularly and wanted to thank me for the pleasure the flowers gave her. Her appreciation meant as much to me as growing the flowers for myself. My involvement in horticulture has stemmed from the fascination of watching others enjoy gardens, as much as from my own enjoyment of plants themselves.

While caring for my marigolds, I first realized how little I knew about gardening. It was ten years before I did much gardening again, and like most beginning gardeners, I read many gardening books, asked lots of questions and tried different plants and techniques myself. I learned the most during the years I spent working in garden centers, answering customers' questions. Many times it felt as though I was doing an examination for school! I also asked many questions of the customers and absorbed much useful information from them.

Working in garden centers, I realized west coast gardeners are eager for more information, and few books are written specifically for our area. Books for all of North America are not always useful in our mild, damp climate, and those written for Great Britain, while by far the most appropriate, sometimes refer to plants and products not available here. This series is written in response to the lack of information for Pacific coast gardeners.

I began research for *Bedding Plants* in the most exciting way known to a keen gardener: I visited the nursery of a friend who was growing unusual bedding plants and bought a few of every type she had. I have always preferred to actually grow something in my own garden before recommending it—a great excuse to try just one more plant!

In addition to growing most of the plants in my own garden, I read gardening books and catalogues, visited public parks and display gardens and asked questions of amateur and professional gardeners and bedding plant growers.

I hope this book will give beginning gardeners the information and encouragement to enjoy gardening, experienced gardeners ideas for new bedding plants and techniques to try and experts a useful reference on this exciting and colorful area of horticulture.

Acknowledgments

Many people and organizations helped in preparing this book, and to them all I offer my most sincere thanks. All are in British Columbia unless otherwise stated.

For the pleasure of allowing us to visit their display gardens and take photographs, thanks go to Minter Gardens, Chilliwack, and Butchart Gardens, near Victoria, and for answering horticultural questions concerning these two facilities, special thanks to Brian Minter and Daphne Fraser.

To Bob Kell, William Choukalos and Karl Chalupa for their patience in allowing strangers into their gardens to take photographs.

To the staff at Ball-Superior Seed Company, Mississauga, Ontario; Ball Seed Co., West Chicago, Illinois; BC Greenhouse Builders, Burnaby; Eddi's Wholesale Garden Supply, Surrey; Fraser Nurseries, Richmond; Green Valley Fertilizer, Surrey; Skagit Nurseries, Mt. Vernon, Washington; and Van Noort Bulb Company, Surrey, for information concerning their products. Special thanks to Tom Linwick and other staff at Molbaks Greenhouse, Woodinville, Washington, for details concerning garden centers in Washington.

To Alex Downie, VanDusen Botanical Garden, Vancouver; Gunter Edel, New Westminster Parks Board; and the gardeners at Stanley Park, Vancouver, for their help in naming cultivars used in photographs.

To Dr. Norma Senn, Fraser Valley Community College, Chilliwack, and All-America Selections Trial Ground Judge, UBC Department of Plant Science, Vancouver; Dr. Gerald Straley, UBC Botanical Gardens, Vancouver; and Dr. Henry Gerber, BC Ministry of Agriculture and Food, Cloverdale, for help with taxonomic and technical details.

To Dr. Robert Armstrong, Longwood Gardens, Pennsylvania for taking the time to share the story of New Guinea impatiens with me; and to Clive Innes, Holly Gate International, Sussex, England, for help with the taxonomy of Livingstone daisy and ice plant.

To George McLauchlan, foreman at Sunset Nursery, Vancouver Parks Board, for giving me information on the best cultivars for the Pacific coast climate and answering many questions on propagation.

To my aunt and uncle, Betty and Terry Myser of Ketchikan, Alaska, for information on gardening in their state.

To my parents, Jack and Dorothy Kent; Darlene Sanders; Claire Bennet and Arthur Rempel; Jim McPhail; Elke and Ken Knechtel; and other friends and associates for help, information and encouragement.

I am grateful to Colleen MacMillan, my publisher at Whitecap Books, for offering me the opportunity to write this book, and to Darby Macnab and the other staff at Whitecap for their support. To Elaine Jones, my editor, for her encouragement, patience and excellent advice.

To my friends Pat Logie and Douglas Justice go my deepest appreciation and admiration. Pat provided me with all of the unusual bedding plants which I had hoped to write about, giving me the opportunity to have hands-on experience with them. On top of that, she answered an endless string of questions about cultivars, propagation and care of bedding plants, particularly in a greenhouse situation. Douglas shared with me his extensive knowledge of all areas of horticulture and his deep love of plants. His generosity in reading the manuscript, his honesty and sense of humor made all the difference.

To my children, Gwyneth, Morgan and Evan, and to my husband, David, for his kind support and for all those early mornings in search of just the right shot before the sun got too bright, while I was fast asleep, I extend my love and gratitude.

Finally, I dedicate this book to the memory of my grandmother, Dorothy Hilda Myser, through whose eyes I first saw gardens as magical places.

Introduction

Our small corner of the continent has a unique climate and, fortunately for gardeners here, it is a great one for gardening. Warmed by the Pacific in winter, cooled by it in summer, our weather is always variable but rarely extreme–no hurricanes or tornadoes, no hot sultry nights with electrical storms, no blizzards which drop feet of snow overnight. Our year is marked by some snow, lots of rain produced when the moist ocean air meets the mountains, maybe a summer with two wet months but more often a good spell of two dry months. Spring and fall always bring surprises: wind, fog and showers and, with luck, some of the wonderful warm days which come in March and October and are loved by all in the Pacific coast region.

What is the Pacific coastal region?

For the purposes of this book, the Pacific coastal region is defined as the area between Alaska and California, west of the Cascade and Coast Mountain ranges. (See map on following pages.) It includes southeastern Alaska,

Plant Hardiness Zones of the Pacific Coastal Region

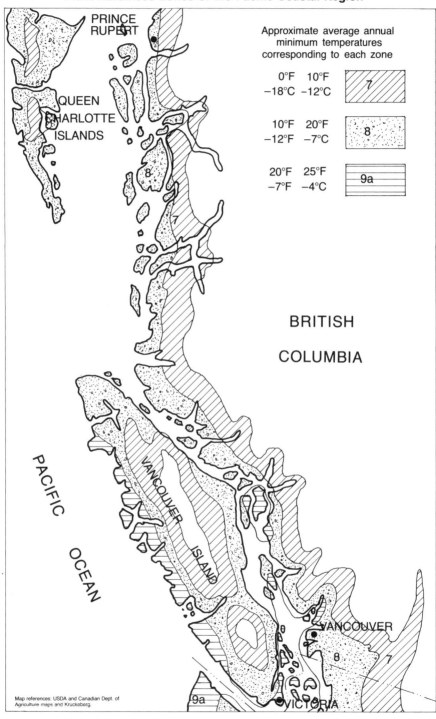

Approximate average annual
minimum temperatures
corresponding to each zone

0°F	10°F	
−18°C	−12°C	7

10°F	20°F	
−12°F	−7°C	8

20°F	25°F	
−7°F	−4°C	9a

PRINCE RUPERT

QUEEN CHARLOTTE ISLANDS

BRITISH

COLUMBIA

PACIFIC

OCEAN

VANCOUVER ISLAND

VANCOUVER

VICTORIA

Map references: USDA and Canadian Dept. of
Agriculture maps and Kruckeberg.

Plant Hardiness Zones of the Pacific Coastal Region

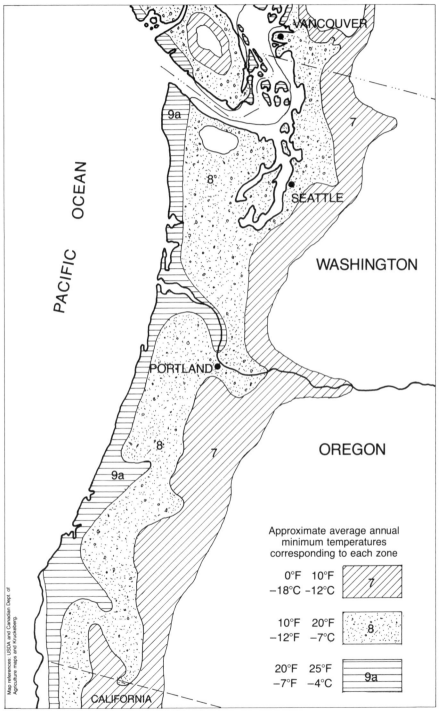

Approximate average annual minimum temperatures corresponding to each zone

| 0°F | 10°F | 7 |
| −18°C | −12°C | |

| 10°F | 20°F | 8 |
| −12°F | −7°C | |

| 20°F | 25°F | 9a |
| −7°F | −4°C | |

Map references: USDA and Canadian Dept. of Agriculture maps and Kruckeberg

coastal British Columbia, Washington and Oregon, and the coastal areas of the islands adjacent to the coast.

North America is divided into ten plant hardiness zones, with 1 being the coldest and 10 the warmest. Within each zone, there is a warmer and colder subzone. The area covered by this book includes plant hardiness zones 7, 8 and 9a (the colder subzone of zone 9). In much of the region, the average rainfall is 60-80 inches (150–200cm) per year. Some areas, such as the Olympic Peninsula, the north coast of BC and southeastern Alaska, receive over 150 inches (375 cm) of rainfall each year and that becomes the limiting factor in which bedding plants do well. The mountains of Vancouver Island and the Olympic Penninsula cause a rainshadow area on the Gulf Islands, the San Juan Islands and the southeast coast of Vancouver Island. In these areas the rainfall is less, averaging 30 inches (75 cm) per year.

Tailored for the Pacific coastal region

This book presents bedding plants that have proven to do well in the Pacific coastal region and gardening information specific to the area. It details all of the plants you are likely to run into in a garden shop and those which you might see in a friend's garden or in hanging baskets and bedding schemes in large public gardens.

Included in the encyclopedia with each entry is a comment on whether you are likely to find plants in garden centers in spring or whether you should plan on growing your own from seed. A list of sources for plants and seed has been included. Please ask for particular varieties at your favorite garden center first; the market is changing quickly as more and more people get excited about gardening, and each season growers are bringing new and interesting cultivars to shops. If possible, ask to speak to the person who does the ordering or leave them a note. Garden centers are very hectic in the spring and if you ask the clerks for a particular plant they may forget to mention it to the buyer. Another excellent source of plant material is gardening clubs, which usually have plant sales as fund raisers. Some of these organizations are listed at the back of the book.

What are
Bedding Plants?

M̲ost gardening book series have one volume about annuals, but the scope of this book is expanded to cover most of the plants you are likely to find in the "bedding plant" section of a garden shop and which you might see used in bedding schemes and hanging baskets in public display gardens. It groups together in one volume those plants that are used for the same purpose in the garden: that is, seasonal color. These plants are temporary on the garden scene, being planted with the intention of removing them at the end of the season. Included are annuals, biennials, perennials, a few plants that are shrubs in their native land, several vines and creepers and some plants that grow from bulbs or tubers.

Unusual annuals that you are not likely to find in shops are also described here. The commercial bedding plant industry is oriented to producing a plant which looks good, preferably in bloom, in May in a 4-inch (10-cm) pot at the largest. There is tremendous price competition, so most suppliers are not willing to grow an unusual crop which might be more expensive to produce or difficult to sell. You might find these unusual bedding plants at a specialty garden center (see the list of sources page 150), but, in most cases, they will have to be grown from seed.

Following are explanations of the various categories of bedding plant referred to in the encyclopedia part of the book. Knowing more about the origins of bedding plants and how they grow in the wild will give you a better understanding of their needs in your garden.

Hardy and half-hardy annuals

An annual is a plant that completes its life cycle in one growing season; that is, it grows, blooms, sets seed and dies all in one year. Examples are sweet alyssum, marigold, and lobelia. Annuals must be propagated from seed, but, unless you intend to save the seed, remove fading flowers to prevent seed from forming. Once annuals set seed, they will stop blooming.

Annuals fall into two groups: hardy and half-hardy. Most of the common hardy annuals are native to Europe, so it is not surprising that they were among the very first flowers cultivated in gardens. It would have been easy to save a bit of seed from a wild plant and throw it into some corner of the garden in the early spring. In their natural life cycle, these hardy annuals bloom in summer and set seed, which drops into the garden, overwinters and sprouts early in the spring. Some may sprout in the fall and the young seedlings will survive the winter and bloom the next spring. All hardy annuals are native to temperate zones and many are the popular "cottage garden flowers," such as cornflowers and love-in-a-mist.

Hardy annuals tend to be easy to grow from seed and do not require any bottom heat to germinate. They may be seeded directly in the garden in March or April and come into bloom quickly. Many will seed themselves in the garden, so watch for seedlings when you weed. Some bloom early and then fade out, whether you deadhead them or not. Cornflowers, candytuft, godetia and annual chrysanthemum tend to do this, but a second sowing will produce bloom later in the summer.

Most of the popular annuals are half-hardy annuals. They are native to the warmer parts of the world and were introduced to Europe by explorers, who brought them home from South Africa, South America, Asia and Australia. You can well imagine that these annuals need some extra care to adapt to our cool weather. Like the hardy annuals, they are grown from seed, but if the seeds are sown in soil which is too cold, they will not germinate. The seeds are generally sown indoors to get earlier bloom. Some require a very warm temperature, which can be provided by setting pots on a heating cable or other heat source. Plants should not be set out until the weather warms up at the end of May or early June. Once established in the garden, they put on a colorful display through the summer.

Half-hardy perennials

Another large group of plants that we use extensively for summer bedding also originates from hot climates, but these plants are actually perennials rather than annuals in their native homes. This means that either some leaves remain on the plant year-round and the plant lives for many years, but does not become woody as a shrub does, or that the leaves die back to ground level, but the roots remain alive (a herbaceous perennial). Unlike an annual, the plant is not "programmed" to set seed and die. They are referred to as half-hardy perennials because they cannot survive the frost.

The fact that they are perennial is not so critical in terms of their use as summer bedding, but knowing their natural inclination is useful in other ways. Many may be propagated from cuttings as well as seed. If a particular plant has some unique feature—for example, the dainty leaves of the geranium 'Distinction'—it may be kept alive indefinitely from cuttings. Named cultivars, which are propagated from cuttings, are actually clones of one original plant; that is, they have identical genes. (Plants grown from seed, although very similar in appearance, are usually variable genetically.) To keep these half-hardy perennials alive from year to year, they must be overwintered in a greenhouse. Those which will tolerate lower light levels, such as fibrous begonias or the polka dot plant, can even be taken indoors for use as houseplants.

Half-hardy shrubs and subshrubs

A handful of bedding plants are actually shrubs or subshrubs from warmer climates. Shrubs form woody branches, while subshrubs are woody just at the base. The interesting feature about the shrubby bedding plants is that because they form woody tissue they have the strength to be trained into tree form, called standards in the nursery trade. Flowering maple, fuchsia and lantana are often trained in this way, and you may see some plants that are over fifteen years old with thick trunks. They are valuable in bedding schemes because they bloom all summer and add height, but they are tricky for the home gardener to overwinter, requiring a cool greenhouse, a sunroom or extra lighting. Fuchsia trees are readily available and not so expensive that it prohibits planting them for one season only.

Biennials

Biennial bedding plants bloom in the second year after they are sown. Some examples are forget-me-nots, wallflowers and sweet williams; they are seeded in summer, planted out in the fall, and after a winter chill they bloom in the second year. Ornamental cabbage and kale fall into this category, but, being grown for foliage alone, the plants are removed before they bloom.

Hardy perennials

Some hardy perennials make excellent bedding plants, for, unlike most perennials, they bloom the first year from seed and continue to bloom most of the summer, two basic requirements for a good bedding plant. A perennial, by definition, will survive the frost and bloom again the following season. The perennials included here are herbaceous perennials—the leaves die down to the ground in winter, but the roots are still alive. Some herbaceous perennials are short-lived and are best started every few years from seed.

Tubers and rhizomes

Four of the bedding plants included are perennials that form tubers or rhizomes. Both are types of swollen roots or stems which function as underground storage organs. These plants may easily be kept from year to year, and some gardeners have tuberous begonias that are over twenty years old.

Using Bedding Plants in the Garden

The first priority when it comes to gardening is that you enjoy it. Whether you have a small balcony garden to dabble in or a large garden to tend, it should meet your personal needs and provide you with pleasure and enjoyment. Consider ideas you get from books and from visiting public and friends' gardens, but don't spoil your fun by imposing others' ideas on your own.

When it comes to designing with bedding plants, you can afford to experiment, because any scheme you don't like will be gone at the end of the season, while favorite arrangements can be repeated year after year. The consequences of planting shrubs or trees in the wrong location are much more serious, but with many bedding plants you can even dig them up and move them during the summer if you are so inclined.

There has been a revival of interest in herbaceous perennials in the past few years and a trend to abandoning traditional bedding plans in favor of more extensive use of perennials. The rationale is that perennials are less work and cost less than buying bedding plants each spring. In fact, though, perennials do require plenty of work and most bloom for about one month, rather than the four or five months that most bedding plants bloom. A combination of both types of plants will offer greater variety, give color through most of the year, reduce cost and still allow experimentation from season to season.

Formal bedding schemes

With the rise of heated greenhouses in Britain in the 1850s, formal bedding-out schemes became the rage. Flower beds with complex outlines were laid out in lawns and filled with bright colors and patterns. These schemes have three components: dot plants for height, groundwork plants for filling in and edging plants to complete the picture. During the late 1800s, there was a movement to replace formal bedding schemes with huge herbaceous borders.

The legacy of these formal bedding schemes is still seen today in public gardens. For example, Figure 7-7 shows a standard lantana used as a dot plant, with groundwork plants of blue salvia, dwarf white marguerites, and red geraniums. Three edging plants are used in neat rows: dwarf yellow marigolds, blue ageratum and white sweet alyssum.

In the home garden, the same orderly effect can be achieved on a smaller scale. Figure 6-10 shows parallel rows of red geraniums and silver dusty miller used to edge a mixed border. A mass of impatiens along a shady front path, a standard fuchsia centered in a circle of begonias, or a bed of snapdragons in a sunny lawn are all echoes of a bygone day.

With formal bedding schemes, it is important to group plants of the same cultivar. To avoid a spotty effect, use large numbers of a few cultivars, rather than a few plants each of many varieties. Formal flower beds are especially effective when situated in a well-tended lawn or with an evergreen hedge as a backdrop.

Bedding plants in the mixed border

The mixed border is an ideal way to use bedding plants in the garden, while taking advantage of the wealth of permanent plant material afforded by the mild Pacific coastal climate. The mixed border consists of a framework of shrubs with spaces, or "bays," for perennials and bedding plants. Shrubs are usually planted toward the back of beds, as most will become tall in time.Combine broadleaf and needle evergreens for year-round texture and add flowering shrubs for summer, winter or fall color. This basic plan will give you an easy-to-care-for framework. In the bays between and at the front of shrubs, plant perennial flowers. Some bloom in winter or early spring before bedding plants; some are unrivalled for flower form and color, lending an air of richness to the garden scene. Bedding plants are the final touch in a mixed border, adding a splash of color in the summer months. The effect of such a well-balanced border is calming and the garden becomes a retreat from the busy pace of daily life.

Bedding plants in a rock garden

A rock garden is really a special type of mixed border, which combines low-growing plants of many types in a sloping setting, accented with large rocks. Rock garden purists prefer plants from high elevations, which are naturally ground-hugging, and would look askance at a rock garden with bedding plants, but experiment and see what works for you. Some suggestions are made in the encyclopedia and any of the "under 1 foot (30 cm) in height" plants from the quick reference chart could be considered.

Specialty gardens

Few gardeners can allot space to a cutting garden as was done in estate gardens, but a row of asters in an out-of-the-way corner or in the vegetable garden will provide masses of cut flowers. Some species, such as zinnias, bloom even more if they are cut.

Providing a child's garden for youngsters is an excellent way to encourage an interest in living things. Children particularly enjoy sweet peas, which they can cut for gifts or set on the table. They like fuchsias because they can pop the flower buds which fill out like balloons, and common flowers such as marigolds, which they recognize in other gardens. Four-o'clocks have big seeds that would be easy for a toddler to handle. Easy-to-grow species with a long bloom time are the best bet for children.

Filling in the gaps in new shrub borders

Newly planted shrubs should be far enough apart that they will not become crowded in a few years, and bedding plants are useful for filling in the gaps in these new shrub plantings. From a design point of view, it is best to use only one or two types of plants for such a purpose. Low-growers such as lobelia, impatiens, alyssum and fibrous begonias are ideal. If taller growers are needed, consider plants such as salpiglossis and cornflower, which have a narrow upright habit. One note of caution: leaves of some shrubs, especially coniferous plants such as false cypress and juniper, will turn brown and their shape will be permanently spoiled if they are crowded by neighboring plants. As summer progresses, trim bedding plants if necessary to prevent crowding.

Container gardens: on the ground or in the air

Bedding plants are sensational in containers, be it hanging baskets, window boxes, planters of cedar, concrete, plastic or terra cotta. An advantage of growing bedding plants in containers is that the scene may be changed with the season. A large Chinese egg pot full of flowers by the front door is dramatic-looking, easy and fairly inexpensive to arrange. For some balcony gardeners, growing bedding plants in containers has become an art. Spring is ushered in with pots of pansies, wallflowers and spring-flowering bulbs, which are replaced with masses of lobelia, marigolds, geraniums and ageratum for all-summer color. In fall, interest is created using ornamental cabbage, dusty miller and perhaps an evergreen shrub. Chapters 5 and 6 are devoted to containers and hanging baskets.

3

From the Plant's Point of View

$\mathbf{A}$n understanding of a plant's biological requirements can assist in getting the most out of your garden. The light a plant needs in order to produce its own food through photosynthesis and the soil in which it will secure its roots and take up water and nutrients are the two most important factors in its environment. Gardening is a combination of putting a plant in the right spot and at the same time modifying its situation through watering, fertilizer and soil improvement. As you work, keep a mental checklist of plant needs, and you will find that your skill and appreciation increases enormously.

Light

This is the most difficult aspect of plant culture to control in the garden, so it is really the limiting factor in what plants you will be able to use in a specific setting.

13

The amount of sun a location receives is usually defined in terms of full sun, half-shade and shade. Full sun is defined as at least four hours of sun during the middle of the day, between about 10 a.m. and 4 p.m. Half-shade is sun during the early morning or late afternoon, or the light received under trees with small leaves, such as birch. Shade cast all day by a building or trees with large leaves is full shade.

However, other factors should be taken into consideration. Reflected light bouncing off a white wall, for example, will brighten an otherwise shady area or turn a sunny location into a baking hot spot, and plants that normally prefer some shade will tolerate more light if the soil is not overly dry or if the area is protected from drying winds.

As with many situations in gardening, often you won't know until you try. If the light factor is not right, your plants will soon let you know. Lack of light will cause the plant to become stretched, the leaves may become thin and the plant will not bloom well. If a plant gets too much sun, the leaves will look bleached or dry and burned-looking. Because they do not have extensive roots, most bedding plants will tolerate being moved, so if you feel the plant is unhappy with a particular sun situation, it is possible to dig it up, with an 8-inch (20-cm) ball of soil, and to replant it in a different location, watering it in well.

When planting under trees, remember that even though the light factor may be right for a shade-tolerant plant, the roots of a tree tend to steal all the moisture and nutrients from the soil. This is especially true of coniferous trees. If you are using bedding plants in such a setting, enrich the soil and be generous with fertilizer. Minter Gardens, a display garden near Vancouver, BC, has lovely displays of impatiens. Both common impatiens and New Guinea hybrids are planted under cedar trees, which have a deserved reputation for being hard to garden under. Liberal amounts of mushroom manure or horse manure with fir shavings are spread below the trees in the fall, and in the spring the impatiens are planted with 6-8-6 organic base fertilizer. The results are outstanding.

To sum up, the first consideration when choosing the plants for any location is light. If you are planning your garden in winter or early spring, be sure to consider the light factor when the sun is higher in the sky and there are leaves on the trees.

Soil

Even a very difficult soil situation, such as the example of cedar trees given above, can be modified to become a successful growing medium. With a little work (or sometimes, to be quite honest, a lot of work), any soil can be improved. The most difficult soil to deal with is one which is poorly drained. Properly, drainage tiles should be laid to improve drainage, but this is very expensive. There are some alternatives to drain tiles on the market, but there is no way to avoid the digging. An easier solution for the home gardener is to construct raised beds or planters. Landscape ties or timbers make this an easy and relatively inexpensive job.

Soils have both a mineral and an organic component. The mineral component is derived from weathered rock. The size of mineral particles contributes to soil texture: many very fine particles result in a clay soil; as particle size increases the soil becomes sandy. This texture determines the rate of flow of water, with water moving slowly through a clay soil. That means it takes a lot of watering to thoroughly wet a clay soil, and it doesn't dry out quickly. A sandy soil needs less water to be wet to the same depth, but it dries out very quickly. To get an idea of which type of soil you have, squeeze a damp handful of soil, then gently press on the ball. If it stays as a firm hard ball, you probably have clay soil; if it crumbles easily, your soil is probably sandy.

Clay and sandy soil differ in their ability to retain plant nutrients. Fertilizer molecules, particularly those of nitrogen and potassium, are easily washed out of sandy soils, but are held in clay soils more firmly, remaining available to plants. If you have a sandy soil, you will use more fertilizer to keep your plants healthy than if you have a clay soil.

The organic component of soil is, by definition, derived from living material. In a woodland, for example, decomposing leaves contribute to the organic matter. In our gardens, we add organic matter in the form of well-rotted manure, compost, peat moss or wood chips. Organic matter improves soil immensely, making clay soil drain more quickly and keeping sandy soil from drying out as quickly. Because it is mostly carbon, decomposed organic matter–humus–darkens the soil, causing it to absorb heat and warm faster in the spring.

Hint: If adding wood chips to soil, mix in 8 ounces (227 grams) by weight of bloodmeal to each 5 pounds (11 kg) of chips. Do not use cedar chips, as they are toxic to plants.

The spongier texture of a soil with plenty of organic matter makes it easier for plant roots to penetrate, so plants will grow faster. In addition, organic matter has the ability to retain fertilizer molecules, of particular benefit to sandy soils.

Soil pH

The pH is a measure of the acidity of a solution and is always expressed as a number from 0 to 14; 7 is a neutral pH. The lower the pH, the more acidic the solution; the higher the pH, the more alkaline. For example, lemon juice has a pH of 2; vinegar, pH 3; beer, pH 4. Milk has a pH of nearly 7; sea water, pH 8; and milk of magnesia, pH 10. Soil pH is determined by mixing the soil with water and measuring the pH of the resulting solution. Gardeners often refer to acidic soils as being sour and to neutral or slightly alkaline soils as being sweet. Depending on the pH of the soil, certain nutrients may exist in unavailable forms or may be present in toxic amounts.

In the Pacific coast region, the high rainfall causes naturally acid soils. At pH of about 5.5 or 5.0, such soils are ideal for acid-loving plants, such as azaleas and rhododendrons. A slightly sweeter soil, about pH 6–7, is better for most of the bedding plants covered in this book. (One exception is the begonia, which can flourish in a pH as acid as 5.5.) At pH 6.5, there is the greatest availability of all soil nutrients.

Ideally, you should test the pH of your soil each year. There are test kits available in shops, garden centers often have soil testing clinics, or you may go to a private soil testing laboratory. Testing results from a laboratory include nutrient levels, pH, salinity and soil texture as well as recommendations for improving soil. For a soil testing lab near you, refer to the yellow pages in the telephone directory, under laboratories–testing. Samples may also be sent to most labs through the mail, if you live out of town. Fees are surprisingly reasonable.

To make your soil sweeter, it is necessary to add lime. There are three liming materials available to the home gardener. Hydrated lime (calcium oxide) is fast-acting and should only be used in preparing new beds before planting, never around existing plant material. Ground limestone (calcium carbonate) is sold as home and garden lime or agricultural lime. It takes from one to three months to act, depending on the particle size of the lime. Dolomite lime (calcium-magnesium carbonate) is ground from limestone high in magnesium, an important plant nutrient and one often deficient in Pacific coast soils, making dolomite the lime of choice. Like calcium carbonate lime, it takes one to three months to act. Wood ashes also make the soil sweeter.

In general, adding 5 lbs. of lime per 100 square feet (11 kg per 9m^2) of soil will raise the pH one point. Do not use more lime than this in one application. If a greater change than one point is necessary, apply twice a year.

For faster results, use hydrated lime at 3½ lbs. per 100 square feet (1.6 kg per 9m²), in new beds only, never near plants. Do not add lime and fertilizer to the soil at the same time; allow at least a week between the two.

Plant nutrients: N, P and K

The three major plant nutrients are nitrogen, phosphorous and potassium. N is the chemical symbol for nitrogen, P is for phosphorous and K is for potassium. The three numbers which must appear on all fertilizers represent the percentage of N, P and K in a standardized reference form. For example, 20-20-20 has the equivalent of 20 percent nitrogen, 20 percent phosphorous and 20 percent potassium.

Nitrogen is important for overall plant health, but especially for the leaves. As explained under soil, nitrogen in the form that is usable by plants is readily washed out of some soils. A deficiency of nitrogen causes the older leaves to turn yellow and the new leaves to become quite small. Too much nitrogen results in dark green leaves, lots of soft leafy growth and few flowers. Excess nitrogen will also depress the amounts of phosphorous and potassium taken up.

Phosphorous is particularly important in root development. Like nitrogen, the available phosphorous washes easily out of some soils. Too little phosphorous will show up as dark green leaves and retarded growth. Leaves may be purplish and drop early. This symptom is often seen in a cold, wet spring. Adding phosphorous to the soil will help the plant cope with cool soil. Too much phosphorous is not usually a problem.

Potassium encourages general plant vigor and maturity. It increases a plant's resistance to disease and cold weather. A deficiency shows up as mottled lower leaves, yellowing beginning at the margin. Serious root injury may result from excessive amounts of potassium.

Minor nutrients

Plants need other nutrients in smaller quantities. Calcium, magnesium, sulfur, iron, manganese, zinc, copper, boron, chlorine and molybdenum all play a role, but, with the exception of magnesium and iron, are unlikely to be deficient in most garden soils. If using soilless potting mixes in containers, however, it is worth adding "fritted trace elements." This fertilizer has trace elements (all those listed above except calcium, magnesium, sulfur and chlorine) with finely ground glass (frit) as a carrier. Calcium is present in lime and both calcium and magnesium in dolomite lime.

Fertilizer application types

There are basically two application types of fertilizer—dry and wet. **Granular fertilizers** are mixtures of dry fertilizers. They are sprinkled on the soil surface, mixed into the top few inches (10 cm) and watered in well. They are easy to use and ideal for making up a flower bed. Adding a formula such as 6-8-6 or 4-10-10 will get plants off to a good start and last for about 4–6 weeks. The application should be repeated in late June and late July.

Soluble fertilizers are liquid or dry concentrates which must be diluted or dissolved in water. They are especially suitable for watering young transplants and container gardens, and take up less storage space than bulky granular fertilizers. Soluble fertilizers are fast acting and give the gardener an opportunity to respond immediately to a plant's needs. At transplant time, use a fertilizer with plenty of phosphorous, such as 10-52-17, to promote root growth. If a plant has too much leafy growth and not enough bloom, use a fertilizer with less nitrogen, such as 15-30-15. If foliage is pale, use more nitrogen, for example, 20-20-20. (Check for spider mites first; they also cause pale foliage.)

Controlled release fertilizers such as Osmocote or Nutricote are the deluxe way to go. Nutrients are released according to the soil temperature, so plants get food when they are growing the fastest. The beauty of controlled release fertilizers is that they last from three months to one year, depending on the preparation. Most widely available to the home gardener is the three month 14-14-14 formulation; applied in late May, it will feed plants through the summer.

Organic fertilizer

Some gardeners prefer to use natural products to provide plant nutrients. The following recipe is a general purpose organic fertilizer. It may be used for vegetable and other garden plants. Omit lime if fertilizing acid-loving plants such as azaleas and rhododendrons. Mix together:

18

- four parts by volume seed meal or fish meal
- one part by volume rock phosphate *or* ½ part bone meal
- one part by volume dolomite lime
- one part by volume kelp meal

While organic fertilizers are a bit more expensive, they are much longer lasting in the soil than chemical fertilizers. As the summer warms up and the activity of soil microorganisms increases, more and more nutrients are released. If used each year, the soil will improve continually.

Planning
and
Planting

There are two basic approaches to planning a garden. In the first, the garden designer decides what picture he or she wishes to achieve and then systematically decides which plants to use. In terms of bedding, the procedure is as follows:

- Decide where in your garden you would like to use bedding plants.
- Make a note of the light and soil conditions, the heights required and the area of ground to be covered.
- Use the quick reference chart to determine possibilities based on height, suggested uses, light and soil.
- Refer to the photographs and read about each possible choice in the encyclopedia to find out more about cultivation, foliage, flower shape and color.
- Estimate the number of plants you need based on the suggested planting distances.
- If you prefer to buy as many plants as possible, buy seeds for only the

hard-to-find varieties. (You may need to ask at your local garden center as to whether they plan to carry the plants you wish to buy.) If you like to grow all your plants from seed, order accordingly.

The second approach starts with the plants and works backwards. It is practiced by many plant collectors. If you would like to grow a certain bedding plant, wander around your garden (mentally or physically) looking for a spot that will meet its needs. This approach may not create such a fine effect in the garden, but it is ideal for the plant lover.

Buying bedding plants

There is a lot of competition in the bedding plant market these days, with grocery stores, hardware stores and even furniture stores getting into the act. If you like to get a good deal, shop carefully. There are advantages to buying in a garden center, even though the price may be higher. The plants are more likely to be labelled as to cultivar, the staff are more knowledgeable and the store should have a better selection. Garden shops are more likely to give their plants better care than grocery or hardware stores, because they have trained staff.

Choose plants which look compact, fresh and have good foliage color. If the plants are too tiny, they may have just been transplanted and will not be rooted yet. (If you do buy such young plants, allow them to grow in the packs for a few more weeks before planting out.) On the other hand, if the plants are too large and leggy in the packs, they may be stressed. Peek under the leaves for pests; yellow leaves may indicate hunger or spider mites.

Commercial bedding plant growers use a constant feeding program of soluble fertilizer in the irrigation system. Once in retail outlets, the plants are rarely fertilized. If the plants are being sold for a very low price (sometimes only a dime per pack over the wholesale price), a retailer is not going to spend money on expensive fertilizers and labor. Ideally, try to buy from a grower-retailer who sells directly to the public. If this is not possible, shop where there is a fast turnover of stock. If plants look like they have been in the store too long, they may be hungry and, with such a fast-growing crop as bedding plants, neglect might mean a permanent setback. Once purchased, plants should be fertilized immediately with half-strength 20-20-20.

While bedding plants have traditionally been sold several to a pack (sometimes called a basket), the trend is shifting to produce plants individually in 4-inch (10-cm) pots. These plants have been cared for in the greenhouse for up to a month longer than those in packs, and therefore sell for a higher price. If you have the budget or have a small garden, they are worth buying for the instant impact.

When to buy

There has been a tendency in recent years, particularly as grocery stores get into the bedding plant market, to sell plants too early. This pressures commercial growers to sell to retailers before plants are properly hardened-off. Plants might also be imported from regions further south and might not be acclimatized to cold weather. The public, enjoying the weeks of warm weather we seem to always get in late March and early April, rushes out and buys bedding plants. Often the weather freezes lightly in late April and plants are lost. Even if it doesn't freeze, the long weeks of cold rainy weather we often get until May can cause plants to rot.

Another consequence of early selling is that some cultivars seem to sell out, so that when the proper planting time arrives, selection is not complete. One way around this is to buy plants in early May and keep them in a cold frame, on a protected patio or in the house at night. Don't forget to fertilize them weekly during this time, using a half-strength solution of 20-20-20.

The best planting time for most bedding is the third or fourth week of May. The exception to this rule is container planting. If you are able to move a hanging basket or planter under cover outdoors—on a covered patio or balcony, for example—until late May, you should be able to plant a few weeks earlier. Details for each species are noted in the encyclopedia section.

Soil preparation

During dry weather in April and early May, prepare the ground for planting. Test soil and adjust pH (see page 16). Using a short-handled fork, loosen soil around weeds and remove them, taking care to remove their roots as well. Spread 2–4 inches (5–10 cm) of organic matter over the soil using the flat side of a leveling rake. Broadcast a general fertilizer such as 6-8-6 or 4-10-10 over the soil at 2–4 lbs. per 100 square feet (1–2 kg per 10 m^2). (If lime has been added, wait a week before adding fertilizer.) Dig fertilizer and organic matter well into the top 10 inches (25 cm) of soil, using a short-handled spade. Remove large stones and break up heavy clods as you dig. Avoid walking on and compacting freshly dug soil; lay a board over the surface to walk on if necessary. Finally, level soil surface with the flat side of your leveling rake again.

Planting

Although it runs contrary to our natures, the best day for transplanting bedding plants is an overcast day or one prior to a rainy spell. If the weather is sunny, transplant in the evening, so plants have a good 18 hours to adjust to the change before the sun blazes again.

Make sure plants are well watered before setting them out. Soak if necessary and let drain. Prepare a watering can with a solution of 10-52-17 or 20-20-20. Turn plants upside down to pop them out of their containers. If they do not just slip out, don't tug. Holding the pot upside-down, rap the rim of the pot on the edge of a table and the plant should loosen enough to slide out. With plants that are planted more than one to a pack, gently pull the soil apart into individual root balls.

This next step is a difficult one. Flowers on plants such as marigolds, snapdragons and zinnias should be removed when plants are set out. Although I had always heard this, I could never bring myself to do it. One year when I set out a bed of marigolds, I accidentally dropped my trowel on several of them, snapping off all the flowers. Those plants promptly doubled in size and produced many more blooms, while the others hardly grew at all. This is hard to do after you have waited months to see some color in the garden, but it makes a tremendous difference.

Using a small trowel, make a hole in the soil and set the plant in it. The plant should be at the same soil level as it was in the container. Fill the hole in and water the plant. Water with the prepared fertilizer solution after you have planted three or four plants, rather than waiting until all your planting is done, which may be several hours later.

Tall growers such as snapdragons, asters and salpiglossis need the support of thin bamboo stakes. Plants which have a floppy habit, such as Swan River daisy and wishbone flower, are best supported with twiggy branches. Use prunings about 8 inches (20 cm) long, placed in the soil around young plants, for them to grow through. (These supports stay in place all season, disappearing as the plants grow up around them.)

Care through the summer

Give lots of water during dry spells and some feeding, depending on what fertilizer you used when planting. If it was a granular fertilizer, sprinkle a little 6-8-6 or 4-10-10 on the beds in late June and again in late July. If you used a 3–4 month controlled release fertilizer, you shouldn't need to supplement it. Watch your plants closely and adjust fertilizer with a soluble plant food if necessary (see page 18).

Plants that tend to become leggy will need to have their growing tips pinched. Refer to the encyclopedia for instructions concerning specific plants and use your own judgement as well. The growing tip is not necessarily where the flower is, which can be confusing; look for new leaves unfurling. This tip is known by biologists as the "apical meristem," meristem being rapidly growing and dividing cells. Whereas animals grow all over, plants grow from meristem tips only. In the axil where a leaf meets a stem, there is usually a bud in waiting, an emergency backup if anything happens to the apical meristem. The apical meristem is "dominant," producing hormones that inhibit growth in the axillary buds, but if you pinch out the apical meristem, the side buds start to grow and the plant becomes very bushy. This is great for plants such as geraniums, because they become full and have many more blooms. This principle can be applied to all pruning practices.

"Deadheading," or removing dead flowers, is important to keep the plants well groomed and to prevent them from setting seed. Once annuals set seed, they will stop blooming.

Gardening in Containers

$\mathcal{C}$ontainer gardening and bedding plants go hand in hand. For apartment dwellers, wonderful effects can be achieved in containers. For dressing up a patio or entrance, they are a natural. The container should be as large as possible, while keeping in scale with the setting.

Containers

The most popular wooden containers for garden use are western red cedar planters and oak whiskey barrels. Cedar planters tend to dry out quickly, so it is worth lining them with black plastic before filling with soil. Staple it down if you have access to a staple gun, and punch two or three holes in the bottom for drainage. Window boxes of less than a foot (.3 m) in width will be difficult to keep watered.

Terra cotta clay pots are very attractive but somewhat less practical. Only the more expensive types are guaranteed to be frost-proof, so leaving them out all winter may be risky, particularly if water cannot drain away freely or if the pot is narrower at the top than at the base. Clay pots dry out very quickly; this is prevented by painting the inside of the pots with a tar emulsion or latex paint before filling them with soil.

Concrete planters are very effective, especially in a setting with contemporary architecture. The most popular glazed ceramic containers are the Chinese dragon pots imported from the Orient. Because they are glazed and very thick, they are generally frost-proof if they have drainage holes. Plastic pots make practical containers; they do not dry out quickly and are inexpensive and long lasting. The minimum size should be about 12 inches (30 cm) across.

Be creative when it come to choosing containers; an eclectic collection of containers can become the focal point of a patio garden.

Potting mix recipes

Never use ordinary garden soil alone in a container. It compacts, with poor results. Either use a packaged potting mix or make up your own. The advantages of making your own are that you know exactly what is in it, you can make it in large quantities and it is less expensive. Following are two recipes for homemade potting mix:

Soilless mix	Mix with some soil
27 quarts (27 L) peat moss	27 quarts (27 L) peat moss
9 quarts (9 L) sterilized sand	4 quarts (4 L) sterilized sand
4 oz. by weight (120 g) dolomite lime	4 quarts (4 L) pasteurized garden soil
3 oz. by weight (90 g) FTE*	4 oz. by weight (120 g) dolomite lime
	3 oz. by weight (90 g) FTE*

* FTE are fritted trace elements (see page 17)

The advantage of adding soil to a mix is that it holds the water and nutrients better than peat or sand, especially if it is a good soil. Sand can be sterilized by boiling, but soil should be pasteurized. The process is as follows. First shake soil through a ¼ inch (.6 cm) screen to remove rocks. Place the soil in a pan to a depth of about 4 inches (10 cm), moisten and cover with aluminum foil. Insert a meat thermometer through the foil into the soil, but not touching the pan and set in the oven at 200°F (93°C) for half an hour. When the soil reaches 180°F (82°C), remove pan from oven. Do not allow soil to become hotter than this temperature, or beneficial bacteria will be destroyed. Pasteurization kills worms, slugs, disease-causing fungi and bacteria, soil insects, most viruses and weed seeds. Even more effective is a treatment in the microwave for ten minutes on full. Turn out onto clean newspapers and allow to cool.

Perlite or vermiculite can be substituted for the sand, especially for hanging baskets where lightness is an asset. Use sand when weight is required to prevent tall plants, such as standard fuchsias, from blowing over. Use coarse builders' sand, not beach sand.

> Note: After measuring peat moss, thoroughly moisten with warm water, squeezing the water through the peat. Never use dry peat in the garden.

Adding fertilizer

The recipes above make a little over one bushel of potting mix (35 L). To this quantity, add one of the following fertilizers:

- 6 ounces by weight (180 g) 14-14-14 Osmocote or Nutricote
- 4 ounces by weight (120 g) granular fertilizer such as 6-8-6
- ¼ cup (60 mL) of the organic fertilizer recipe given on page 18–19.

What, when and how to plant

Most bedding plants may be grown in containers. Refer to the quick reference chart under the heading "containers" and the encyclopedia section for suggested plant material.

Most summer-flowering bedding plants should be planted during the last week of May; exceptions are noted in the encyclopedia section. Containers can be planted several weeks earlier if they are under cover of a balcony or if you can move them indoors on nights that promise to be clear and cold.

Fall and winter bedding plants can be planted in September or October. This is also the time to add a few spring-flowering bulbs for a pick-me-up in April.

If your container is very deep and you do not want the weight of a full depth of soil, a foot (30 cm) of vermiculite or perlite can be added to the bottom of the container. Fill the container up to within a few inches (5 cm) of the rim with potting mix. Planting techniques are described on page 24.

Care through the season

The smaller the container, the more care it requires in terms of watering and fertilizing. A small planter box will need water perhaps twice a day by the end of the summer. There are a number of crystals on the market made out of compounds that absorb many times their weight in water and hold it as a reservoir for the plant roots. Although they are still somewhat experimental, greenhouse growers report that the addition of these crystals to the potting mix cuts down on the frequency of watering, making them a useful addition to container plantings.

Fertilizer required through the summer will depend on what type was used in the mix. Controlled release and organic fertilizers will feed plants for several months and need not be repeated. If granular fertilizer was used in the mix, apply more in late June and again in late July, sprinkling ⅓ ounce by weight over each square foot (or 100 g per m²) of soil surface. If you prefer, use a half-strength soluble fertilizer every week (see page 18). Remove faded blooms and pinch the tips of plants to encourage bushiness.

6

Hanging Baskets
and
Moss Baskets

A well-grown hanging basket enriches a setting in a way few other decorations can rival. The city of Victoria on Vancouver Island is famous for its magnificent moss baskets, which hang from blue and white lamp standards, and many other cities are also gracing their streets with these masses of bloom.

Hanging baskets are a specialized type of container garden, so all of the same considerations mentioned in Chapter 5 apply. The larger the container, the greater the ratio of soil volume to surface area. In terms of hanging baskets, this means many plants can be planted and there will still be an adequate volume of soil to ensure root health. It also means that the larger the container, the slower the rate of surface evaporation—less watering for you. So remember, bigger is better when it comes to hanging baskets.

Buying ready-made hanging baskets

In the spring, it seems like every retail outlet sells hanging baskets. Some are gorgeous, in full bloom in late May and packed with top-quality plants nurtured since January; these are a worthwhile investment.

Others are inexpensive, using small pots and few plants. For the same price you could make a larger hanging basket filled with interesting plants in your choice of colors. Baskets you make yourself may not be in full bloom until June, but are better in the long run than poor quality ready-made baskets.

When buying ready-made baskets, sprinkle 1 tablespoon (15 mL) of granular or slow-release fertilizer on the soil surface and water well.

Containers

Most hanging baskets are planted in containers of wood, plastic, clay, pulp or wire. Western red cedar is the best wood for hanging baskets. The standard cedar basket is 12 inches (30 cm) square at the top and the sides taper to form a 4-inch (10-cm) square at the bottom. If you are making your own, it would be much better to make them larger and not so sharply tapered, allowing for more soil volume. Holes are drilled in the side ½ inch (1 cm) from the rim to attach wires. Before you plant your cedar basket, line theinside with black plastic, stapling it down if you can, and punching two or three holes in the bottom for drainage. This way the soil will not dry out as quickly.

Plastic hanging baskets are most often available in green, white and terra cotta red. Fancier pots in a wider selection of colors are sold in large garden centers. The minimum size to buy is 10-inch (25-cm); 12-inch (30-cm) baskets are also manufactured—try asking your garden center (early in the season) to order some if they're not in stock.

Clay pots either have holes in the pot to attach rope or they can be hung in a rope holder. Clay pots dry out very quickly and should be coated inside with black tar emulsion or latex paint.

Pulp pots, made out of dark gray fiberboard, are the least expensive and yet many gardeners feel they are quite attractive, being more natural looking than plastic. They last two or three years, longer if the inside is coated with varathane or latex paint.

Hanging baskets with one type of plant

Plants such as impatiens, fuchsia, ivy geranium, browallia, calceolaria, lotus vine, petunia and hanging basket tuberous begonia are outstanding in hanging baskets when planted alone. In a ten-inch (25-cm) basket, it is best to use 5 or 6 plants, one in the middle and the others around it. If plants are purchased in 4-inch (10-cm) pots, they will fill the basket up faster.

Mixed baskets

When it comes to making a mixed basket, anything goes. A classic combination for a square cedar or pulp basket is as follows:

- Use an upright geranium in the center of the basket.
- Plant two ivy geraniums in opposite corners.
- Plant two trailing fuchsias in the two remaining opposite corners.
- In the four spaces left along the sides plant any of the other plants suggested in the encyclopedia or the quick reference chart. Favorites include trailing lobelia, nepeta and schizanthus.

The delight of planting your own hanging basket is that it may be customized to your light situation or your preferred color scheme. A hanging basket for a shady place in a pastel color scheme might be planted with the upright pink fuchsia 'Miss California', 2 'Pink Marshmallow' fuchsias, 2 schizanthus, 2 mauve ivy geraniums, a green and white variegated English ivy and a green and white wandering Jew.

For a hanging basket in lots of sun, using a bright color scheme, the following combination would work well: an upright red geranium, 2 yellow calceolaria, 1 nasturtium, 1 creeping zinnia, 1 lotus vine, 1 trailing lobelia, and a black-eyed-susan vine.

Planting conventional hanging baskets

If you have a greenhouse or a sunroom, plant your hanging basket in March or April. If you will be placing the basket outdoors, but can leave it under cover for a month (a carport or covered patio for example), you could plant it up in early May. If it goes straight outdoors, don't plant until late May.

Information on buying bedding plants and recipes for potting mixes is given in chapters 4 and 5. To plant up the basket, first water all the plants well and allow them to drain. Fill the basket about two-thirds full of potting mix.

Remove the plants from their pots (see page 24) and gently place them where you wish them to go in the basket. Fill in the spaces between them with more potting mix, making sure that the plants are at the same soil level as they were in their pots. Firm the soil gently and water the basket with a solution of 10-52-17 starter fertilizer.

There is a trick to attaching the wires for hanging baskets, which makes leveling the basket a simple operation. Hold the wires together in your hand and give them one bend together, so they will all be the same length. Then attach each one to a side of the basket, making sure the sharp ends are tucked into the soil to prevent injuries.

Planting moss-lined wire baskets

Moss baskets are much more expensive to buy because of the labor involved, so this is where you can really benefit from making your own. They are easy to make once you know how. To begin, you need a wire basket and a bag of moss. Again, a larger basket is better. They are manufactured in 2-inch (5-cm) increments from 8 inches to 28 inches (20–71 cm). You may have to order the larger sizes through your garden center, but do so early in the season. They are manufactured with round bottoms and flat bottoms, but the latter are easier to work with.

The advantage of moss baskets over conventional hanging baskets is that they are "side-planted." This gives a much greater surface area over which to plant, and because the plants can be seen before they actually get long enough to trail, you can use plants that are less trailing in habit. Figure 1-4 shows a moss basket which is planted with upright tuberous begonias, and Figure 8-6 shows a mixed moss-lined wire basket. Dwarf marigolds, sweet alyssum, viscaria, fibrous begonias, ageratum–almost any dwarf bedding plant–may be used. Moss baskets give you a chance to be your most creative!

Many moss baskets used in public parks and gardens have a large saucer attached to the bottom, which keeps them from drying out as quickly. Wire baskets for home gardeners do not come with attached saucers, but you can easily attach one yourself. A 14-inch (36-cm) wire basket sits nicely in a 7-inch (18-cm) plastic saucer. Make 4 holes in the saucer by heating up a skewer on the stove and pushing it into the plastic ¼ inch (.6 cm) down from the rim. The saucer may then be wired onto the basket after it is planted. If a green saucer is used it will not be very noticeable and will not be visible once the plants grow longer.

The first step is to line the basket half-way up with a layer of moss 1 inch (2.5 cm) thick. If a saucer will not be attached to the basket later, cut a circle of plastic about 12 inches (30 cm) across and press it into the bottom of the basket on top of the moss. This will serve the same purpose, but doesn't store as much water. Now fill the basket about half-full of soil. If the basket is round on the bottom, set it on an empty pot so it won't roll around.

A 14-inch (36-cm) wire basket is usually constructed with four vertical wires soldered to nine circular wires, making 32 openings in the basket. Because the basket tapers, the openings near the top are wider. In a 14-inch (36-cm) basket, plant approximately 16 plants on the sides and 8 in the top opening, spacing them evenly. (If 16 plants are used, only half of the holes will be planted.)

Start planting into the holes about two rows up from the bottom of the basket. To plant into the sides, pull apart two wires to enlarge the hole. Pull back the moss and poke the roots of the bedding plant through the hole. Push the moss back across the hole and bend the wires back the way they were. Clearly this only works with plants grown in packs; a plant in a 4-inch (10-cm) pot would have too large a root ball to side-plant.

As you work your way up the basket, add more moss lining and soil. At the top there is room to use some plants with larger root balls, such as fancy begonias grown from tubers or 4-inch (10-cm) pot plants.

Attach wires as described above under "Planting conventional hanging baskets" and water the basket well with a solution of 10-52-17 starter fertilizer.

Care of hanging baskets through the summer

Water your hanging baskets diligently during hot weather. Small baskets may need to be watered twice a day. If the basket is not too heavy, take it down and soak the whole basket in a tub of water for an hour or so.

Fertilizer required through the summer will depend on what type was used in the mix. Controlled release and organic fertilizers will feed plants for several months and need not be repeated. If granular fertilizer was used in the mix, apply more in late June and again in late July, sprinkling ⅓ ounce by weight over each square foot (or 100 g per m²) of soil surface. If you prefer, use a half-strength soluble fertilizer every week (see page 18). Remove faded blooms and pinch the tips of plants to encourage bushiness.

Propagation

Propagation refers to any technique that will increase the number of plants on hand (buying them doesn't count!). For some gardeners, especially those with greenhouses, starting a new plant from a seed or cutting is a source of great satisfaction. One of winter's pleasures is poring over seed catalogues and planning what new plants to try next season. Other gardeners prefer to leave propagation to someone else.

Seeding is the most common technique for starting the majority of bedding plants and is much more economical than buying plants, a consideration if large numbers are needed. Some cultivars are easy to start from seeds; others require bottom heat, extra light and up to six months to be ready to plant out in late May. There are some cultivars which resent transplanting and should be sown directly into the garden.

Propagation from cuttings is the best method for many bedding plants–a good-sized plant in bloom can be produced in less time than from seed. For named cultivars, such as the fuchsia 'Swingtime' or the geranium 'Distinction', propagation from cuttings is the only way to produce an exact replica of the original plant. Many gardeners, particularly in garden clubs, enjoy swapping cuttings.

The few bedding plants which are hardy perennials form clumps and can simply be divided. Plants that form tubers and rhizomes can also be divided.

Particular details for seeding, making cuttings and division are given with each entry in the encyclopedia section, but the basic techniques are outlined in this chapter.

Starting bedding plants indoors from seeds

Dates to sow are given under each entry in the encyclopedia section. Most bedding plants are sown indoors in March. Slow-growing plants such as begonias and geraniums are seeded in December or January. Start the following in February: snapdragons, canna lilies, cigar flower, carnations, gazanias, lantana and lobelia. You can wait until April for China asters, celosia, globe amaranth and nasturtiums. Ornamental cabbage and kale, wallflowers, forget-me-nots, pansies and primulas, grown for winter bedding, are sown in June.

Seedlings are subject to attack by a number of damping-off fungi (see page 45). To prevent such attacks, hygiene is of the utmost importance. If reusing pots, disinfect them by soaking them in a solution of detergent and one part laundry bleach to ten parts hot water. Particularly sensitive plants should be watered with a fungicide after seeding.

Sowing the seeds. If many seeds are to be sown, use flats—rectangular boxes of wood or plastic. For smaller numbers of seeds, use 6- to 10-inch (15- to 25-cm) azalea pots (pots that are wider than they are deep). For large seeds or seedlings that will remain in their pots from sowing until they go into the garden, use individual 2- to 3-inch (5- to 7.5-cm) pots. Flats of 240 1s—24 thin plastic pots joined as one unit—are also handy. They may be inserted into an ordinary plastic flat for strength and ease of carrying.

Use only sterilized potting mix, either purchased or homemade. If making your own mix, use the recipe on page 28, adding ¾ ounce (21 g) by weight superphosphate. (Do not add other fertilizers to a seeding mix.)

Fill container with potting mix to within ¼ inch (.6 cm) of the rim, gently pressing it down. Sow seeds as specified in the encyclopedia section under each entry. Water with lukewarm water using a watering can with a "seedling rose," which makes a very fine spray; start the flow of water over another container and move the watering can so it sprinkles on the seeded mix when it is flowing evenly. Or set the container in a pan of lukewarm water until the surface of the mix is wet. Allow to drain well and cover with glass or clear plastic if specified; if the containers are in direct sunlight, cover the glass with a sheet of paper to minimize temperature fluctuations. Do not overwater, as more seedlings damp off from overwatering than fail from too little water.

Soil temperature remains 10 degrees cooler than the temperature in a room and some crops need 70°F (21°C) to germinate, which is not possible in a normally heated home. One solution is to purchase a heating cable. The least expensive ones have a thermostat set at 70°F (21°C), which is perfect. (Commercial growers prefer a thermostat they can control, which is much more expensive.)

To use a heating cable, first make a wooden box out of cedar or all-weather wood. Lay the cable on the bottom, arranging it so that it snakes back and forth across the bottom of the box. Secure it with insulated staples. Put a 1-inch (2.5-cm) layer of perlite or vermiculite over the cable. Pots and flats may then be set directly into the box. Keep the containers close together to conserve heat when the cable is on. If directions in the encyclopedia state "germination at 60–70°F (15–21°C)," use of a heating cable is optional, but it will give better results. If only 70°F (21°C) is mentioned, that temperature is required for good results and a heating cable should be used. The top of some refrigerators are warm and may be used to germinate seeds. Another alternative for seeds which require dark and warm soil is to put them near the hot water tank. Hardy annuals normally germinate at cool temperatures and need no bottom heat.

If directions indicate flats should be covered with glass or plastic to conserve moisture and heat, be sure to remove it once seeds germinate.

The **first transplanting** of the seedlings from the seed tray to an individual pot (called pricking out by the British), gives each plant room to develop and access to a potting mix which includes more fertilizer. Seedlings are generally transplanted when the one or two sets of true leaves appear. The first leaves to appear on a seedling are actually not true leaves but are "seed leaves" which were in the seed and contain stored food. These seed leaves will shrivel up and fall off as the true leaves take over the job of providing the young plant with food through the process of photosynthesis. You will recognize the true leaves as they have the characteristic shape of the mature plant.

Seedlings may be transplanted into 1201s–12 thin plastic pots (packs) joined as one unit. Plant four to each pack, the way they are sold in shops. Better still, transplant into individual 2- to 4-inch (5- to 10-cm) pots. This way the intermingled roots won't be pulled apart when planting-out time comes. Use sterilized potting mix but, whether it is your own mix or one from the store, add fertilizer as described on page 29. (Commercial mixes do not contain fertilizer unless stated on the label.) When transplanting, hold each seedling by its seed leaves and lift it from the soil with a dibber or fork. Make a hole in the potting mix and lower the roots into the hole, keeping the plant at the same level it was in the seed tray. Gently firm the soil around the roots and water gently.

Some plants stay in the same pots from the time they are sown until they are planted out into the garden. Remember to use a balanced soluble fertilizer with these seedlings once they have true leaves, as the seeding mix contained only phosphorous.

Hardening off is the process whereby the seedlings are gradually acclimatized to the weather outdoors. Two weeks before the planting-out dates, set them under a cloche or cold frame outdoors, or put plants out during the day and bring them in at night.

Starting bedding plants from seeds outdoors

Seeds of many plants can be sown directly in the garden. The advantages are less fuss indoors and less expense; the main disadvantage is later bloom. Prepare soil as described on pages 23–24. Cover the bed with 1 inch (2.5 cm) of soil that has been sifted through a ¼ inch (.6 cm) sieve. Sow the seeds and cover with a layer of sifted soil that is approximately the thickness of the seeds. Water gently.

> **What are F_1 hybrids?** These are plants which are the result of a careful cross between two parent plants. F_1 hybrid bedding plants are more uniform, vigorous and are generally superior plants. Due to extra handling, seeds are a bit more expensive. Seeds collected from F_1 hybrids will not be true to the parent; if you intend to save your own seeds, bear this in mind.

Making stem cuttings

Bedding plants that are half-hardy perennials, shrubs or subshrubs may be propagated by cuttings. New plants then become clones of the parents, that is, they have exactly the same genes. Plants with outstanding character-istics, such as the popular double red and white fuchsia 'Swingtime', are named and must be propagated from cuttings to be true. Some plants grow faster or bloom sooner from cuttings. Plants which are often grown from cuttings include fuchsia, geranium, marguerite, flowering maple, coleus, felicia, nepeta, English ivy, heliotrope, silver nettle vine, lotus vine, ice plant, osteospermum, wandering Jew, New Guinea impatiens, trailing ver-bena, and lantana.

The ideal time of year to make cuttings is in August or September. Using a razor blade, cut below the fourth leaf joint on a shoot. Pinch off any flower buds and the bottom two leaves or sets of leaves. This will give two nodes (leaf joints) above the soil and two in the soil, where new roots will form. In late summer, a rooting compound is not necessary.

Several cuttings can be rooted in a 6- to 10-inch (15- to 25-cm) azalea pot, or they may be rooted individually in 2- to 4-inch (5- to 10-cm) pots. Fill pots with a mixture of half peat and half perlite or vermiculite and press down gently. Water well and allow to drain. Make holes for the cuttings with a pencil; never use the cutting to make the hole.

Insert the cutting into the hole and water with a fungicide. Keep in a bright place but out of direct sunlight. Lightly mist the leaves twice a day and water when the soil surface becomes dry. Cuttings root in about ten days and, once rooted, should be fertilized with half-strength soluble 10-52-17 starter fertilizer. If several cuttings were made in one pot, they should be transplanted into individual 4- to 6-inch (10- to 15-cm) pots af-ter one month.

Growing under lights

It is difficult to grow sturdy seedlings indoors without extra light, unless you have a sunroom. Extra light should be provided using two fluorescent tubes—one cool white and one warm white—4 to 6 inches (10–15 cm) from the plants. Such a light arrangement would also allow you to overwinter cuttings of suitable bedding plants without them becoming stretched and weak. If you do not have extra lights, consider delaying seeding for a few weeks from the recommended sowing time to reduce the amount of time seedlings spend indoors. There is also more light later in the spring, mak-ing even a window sill a brighter place to grow.

Pests
and
Diseases

The following are the most common pests and diseases that you are likely to encounter in the garden; only a few greenhouse pests and diseases have been included because there are so many. If a problem does not fit one of the following descriptions, take a sample (or a photo) into your favorite garden center and ask for help. In British Columbia, Oregon and Washington, the law requires that anyone giving pesticide advice be a licensed pesticide dispenser. The excellent reference book *A Gardener's Guide to Pest Prevention and Control in the Home and Garden* is available for a small fee from: BC Ministry of Agriculture and Food, Parliament Buildings, Victoria, BC, V8W 2Z7.

If using any pesticides, please remember the following:

- Only use an insecticide if damage is seen. Do not spray regularly to prevent insect pests.
- As a first choice, use an insecticidal soap or an organic pesticide.
- Always read the label very carefully and follow instructions exactly.

- Wear rubber gloves and long sleeves and trousers.
- Do not spray when the bees are out foraging. The best time of day is just before the sun sets.
- Do not spray unless the air is still.
- Do not spray if you have any health problems or are pregnant.
- Store all chemicals and fertilizers out of the reach of children and pets in a locked box or cupboard.
- Do not spray with chemicals indoors; always take the plants outdoors.

APHIDS are insects with soft, pear-shaped bodies, which cluster in large numbers near the ends of new shoots and under leaves, causing them to curl. Usually green, gray or pink, they suck the sap of plants and produce a sweet substance called "honeydew." Ants often "farm" aphids, carrying them to infest new plants and collecting the honeydew. If you see an army of ants marching up and down a plant's stems, look for aphids. Because aphids suck the sap, they may transmit viral diseases from plant to plant. Ladybird beetles and their young prey on aphids; take care not to harm them. If there are only a few aphids, they may easily be rubbed off the plant by hand. Or use an insecticidal soap (except on nasturtiums or sweet peas), rotenone or an all-purpose insecticide such as malathion.

ASTER WILT is caused by the pink fungus (*Fusarium* sp.), which clogs up the water-conducting vessels in the plant. Young plants may suddenly collapse and die. On more mature plants, the leaves may turn yellow and wilt, beginning with the lower leaves. A thin coating of pink spores may be seen on the lower stem. There is no treatment and the plant should be removed. The disease persists in the soil and may be transmitted on shoes or tools. Do not throw diseased plants in the compost and do not plant China asters in the same place twice.

CABBAGE BUTTERFLY is dainty and white or pale yellow. It flutters around cabbages, where it lays eggs that hatch into green caterpillars up to 2 inches (5 cm) long. They are hard to spot because they lie along the midrib of the leaf, but they can munch a lot of cabbage in a short time. Hand pick if possible. A spray containing B.T. (*Bacillus thurengiensis*) is harmless to other creatures but contains a bacterium which infects and kills the caterpillars. Some books recommend Sevin, but it is extremely toxic to bees.

CATERPILLARS There are numerous caterpillars found in the garden. They are all the larval stage of moths and butterflies and most feed on leaves. B.T. (*Bacillus thurengiensis*) is the pesticide of choice. See also cabbage butterfly caterpillars, above, and cutworms, below.

CLUB ROOT is a disease caused by a fungus in the soil. It infects many members of the family Brassicaceae: broccoli, Brussels sprouts, cauliflower, kale, cabbage, stocks and wallflowers, and is more prevalent on acid, poorly drained soil. Lime well where these crops are to be grown. Some gardeners advise never to buy young plants of these crops to avoid bringing the fungus in with the soil. Once the fungus is in the garden, there is little to be done to get rid of it, except to wait it out. Do not grow plants from this family for up to five years if your soil has club root.

CUTWORMS are a type of large caterpillar which inhabits the upper layers of soil. Cutworms have soft bodies that are not fuzzy, and they curl up when disturbed. They feed at night, often cutting the base of a plant so it falls over completely. Or, as with cleome, they will eat a ring around the base of the stem, which causes the plant to weaken and die. They may also climb up to the top of plants such as tomatoes and eat holes in the fruit, returning to the soil by daylight. For large plants, such as cleome, place a collar of tar paper around the base of the stem. For more closely planted varieties such as fibrous begonias, use B.T. (*Bacillus thurengiensis*) or sprinkle granular diazinon on the soil surface and water in.

DAMPING-OFF refers to a fungal attack which results in seeds failing to emerge or in the collapse of young seedlings. Always sow seeds in sterilized soil and do not sow too thickly. Once seedlings emerge, grow on at the recommended temperature and provide good air circulation. If noted in the encyclopedia that damping-off is a particular problem, a suitable fungicide should be used. Ask at your garden center, as recommendations for fungicides are changing.

DRY BROWN PATCHES on the leaves are most often caused by too little water, although chemical damage must be considered if plants have been sprayed.

EARWIGS are dark brown insects about 1 inch (2.5 cm) long with forceps-like pincers at the rear. They are most often found hiding in dahlias, where they sometimes eat the flowers and leaves. To trap earwigs, stuff newspaper into the bottom of a clay flower pot and invert over a wooden stake near the damaged plants. The paper can then be burned each day.

FLEA BEETLES are tiny, ⅛-inch (.3-cm), black beetles that are hard to spot because they jump like fleas. Damage—tiny holes in the leaves—is usually not serious enough to warrant attention; plants will normally outgrow the damage. If flea beetles are a cause for concern, use rotenone dust or spray.

GRAY MOLD (*Botrytis*) is one of the most common of all fungal diseases, partly because spores are carried in the air. The disease may affect any plant part, but is most common on old flowers and leaves in humid conditions. Keeping the garden well groomed will help control the disease. Treatment with a fungicide may help, but if the weather is extremely wet and cold, there is little that can be done.

LEAFHOPPERS are small insects related to aphids and, like them, suck the plant sap. Unlike aphids, they jump and fly off the plants when disturbed. They feed on the undersides of leaves and shed their cast skins, a sign that they are present. While direct damage to plants is slight, they may transmit serious viral diseases. Spray with Ambush or an all-purpose insecticide such as malathion.

LEAF REDDENING is a sign of too-cold temperatures in the spring. It often indicates a deficiency of phosphorous, which is taken up poorly in cold weather. With the onset of warmer weather, leaf color will improve.

MEALY BUGS may infest flowering maples indoors or in the greenhouse. They are tiny, white, wooly insects which look like bits of fluff. They are usually found at the axil of stem and leaf and, like aphids, suck the plant sap. Kill them by dabbing them with a cotton swab dipped in rubbing alcohol, or spray with insecticidal soap.

OEDEMA is a fluid imbalance within a plant; it happens most often in late winter to greenhouse geraniums. The plants are given more water than they can get rid of, which results in blisters forming on the underside of the leaves. These rupture and form reddish, corky scabs. Generally this is of little concern, but it is best to maintain good air circulation and water only in the morning and not too much, especially in overcast weather.

PHYSIOLOGICAL DISORDERS are not caused by disease organisms, but instead indicate less than ideal conditions of water, fertilizer or light. (LEAF REDDENING and OEDEMA are examples.) Refer to the cultural instructions to determine the problem and possible changes in plant care to alleviate it.

POWDERY MILDEW is a fungus disease which leaves a white, powdery coating on leaves and shoots. It appears most often during warm, muggy summer weather. Plants are also more susceptible if the soil is allowed to dry out. Try not to wet foliage when watering. Spray every two weeks with benomyl or sulfur.

ROOT WEEVIL adults are dull, gray-black beetles with a distinctive long snout. (Do not confuse them with shiny, black ground beetles which are very beneficial in the garden.) They eat the margins of primula leaves and, unfortunately, are hard to eliminate. Generally primulas tolerate a moderate amount of weevil damage. Of serious concern is damage to rhododendrons and other woody plants. The weevil larvae eat the roots and girdle plant stems, eating around them at the base. This will easily kill a large shrub. In fact, some gardeners recommend planting primroses under rhododendrons to give the weevils something else to eat. To kill weevils, try a diazinon soil drench.

ROTS include root rots, stem rots and basal rots. It is a general term used for fungal diseases which cause plant tissue to become black and soggy. In seed trays, it may be prevented by using sterilized potting mix and not overwatering. In the garden, rots are due to planting out too early and there is no practical cure.

RUST appears most often on snapdragons and sweet williams. As with many plant diseases, healthy plants are most resistant. The symptoms are reddish brown spots on the underside of the leaves. Plants which look healthy and are in full bloom may reveal a coating of rust spots under their leaves if one peeks. Although snapdragons usually bloom until the frost, infected plants will be ruined by about August and need to be removed. If desired, spray with sulphur. Rust is a fungus.

SCALE insects are sometimes difficult to spot. On bedding plants, they are most common indoors or in the greenhouse. They appear as brown, yellow or white bumps on the stems. Poked with a fingernail, they will pop off the stem. These "bumps" hide mature scale insects; eggs are laid and the young crawl around and settle down in a new location. If the infestation is serious, the time to spray with rotenone or malathion is at this "crawler" stage, which you will have to look for. For most infestations, hand picking or dabbing each scale with rubbing alcohol will be just as easy as spraying, and much safer and less expensive.

SLUGS and **SNAILS** are mollusks, related to clams, limpets, moon snails and other aquatic animals bearing shells. Slugs have rudimentary shells and are certainly not as handsome as their cousins. They both do a tremendous amount of damage in gardens, eating seedlings right off at ground level and eating leaves all summer. Look for the glistening trails to be sure the damage is from slugs and not cutworms or caterpillars. The most common slug and snail baits are bran-based and thus are very attractive to pets and toddlers, especially the pellet types. Use with extreme caution, setting the bait in an upside-down, empty plastic container with one hole cut in the side and placing a heavy rock on top so it cannot be overturned. Liquid slug baits are also effective. A "slug fence" is available which is made of salt and is completely non-toxic.

SPIDER MITES are a serious pest in the garden and indoors. They are difficult to spot because they are minute. A telltale sign is the yellowing of older (bottom) leaves or a pale dusty look to the foliage. Often leaves fall without even looking unhealthy. If you look under leaves, you may be able to see fine webbing, but it is best to use a magnifying glass to detect the mites themselves. If you watch carefully you can see them walking around. If you see tiny specks on the leaves, poke them to see if they run away—a sure sign they aren't dust! Control is difficult. Try insecticidal soap weekly for several weeks or use a miticide which contains dicofol.

VIRUS organisms are made up of genetic material and are not organized into cells as are other living organisms. There is debate as to whether they are "life" as we usually think of it, but they certainly have the ability to affect normal cell functions. Because they are inside the plant cells, there is no way to kill them without killing the plant. A plant that shows symptoms of a virus disease should be destroyed. Virus particles are spread from plant to plant by sap-sucking pests such as aphids. Symptoms include abnormal growth such as stunting, deformed leaves and yellow streaks or rings on the leaves. Interestingly, the attractive variegation of the flowering maple, *Abutilon pictum* 'Thompsonii', is caused by a virus which does not harm the plant.

WHITEFLY is a serious pest in the greenhouse, and may be introduced into your garden with plants grown in a greenhouse. They are tiny delicate white flies which hide under leaves and flutter about when the plants are moved. In the greenhouse, try one of the following:

- Trap flies with automotive STP oil painted onto an 8-inch (20-cm) square of cardboard hung near plants.
- Spray with permethrin or insecticidal soap weekly for several weeks.
- Burn an insect coil.

In the garden, spray with an insecticide containing permethrin, such as Ambush.

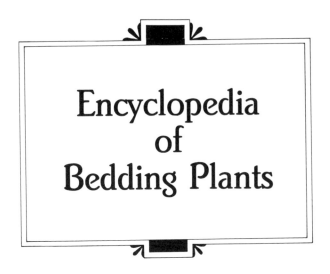

Encyclopedia of Bedding Plants

The following encyclopedia gives information on 122 bedding plants, with a description including height and bloomtime; origin and history; cultural details regarding light and soil and how to grow; and suggested uses in the garden. It is organized alphabetically according to botanical names and cross-referenced with common names. Only instructions specific to each entry are given; for general information, please refer to the opening chapters.

How plants are named

The international organization for plant nomenclature–Taxon–assigns plants their botanical names and makes changes as required. Although often referred to as Latin names, many have Greek roots. Botanical names seem intimidating at first, but with practice they become more comfortable to use. The following example explains the meaning of the various names and how they are distinguished.

Glechoma hederacea 'Variegata' (*Nepeta hederacea*) "nepeta" LAMIACEAE

The first name (*Glechoma*) is the name of the genus to which this plant belongs (the generic name). A genus (plural genera) is a group of plants which are closely related. In some cases, as the above example illustrates, the generic name has also become the common name. Other examples are begonia, chrysanthemum, coleus, dahlia and fuchsia.

The second name (*hederacea*) is the name of the species to which the plant belongs (the specific name). Names of both genus and species are either italicized or underlined (unless being used as a common name). A multiplication sign (x) at the beginning of the species name indicates that it is not in fact a true species, but a hybrid between two or more species. The x is neither italicized nor pronounced.

Some plant species have naturally occurring subgroups which are consistently distinct enough to warrant an additional designation—subspecies, variety or forma. For example, *Amaranthus hybridus* var. *erythrostachys* is a variety found in the wild.

In the above example, 'Variegata' is the cultivar name and is not underlined or italicized, but is enclosed in single quotation marks. A cultivar is a variety originated and maintained by humans, and of botanical or horticultural importance, requiring a name. Such a plant would not usually be found in the wild. Many of these names are well known: 'Twinkles' impatiens, 'Bicentennial' fuchsia and 'Vodka' begonias are examples. Since 1959, new cultivar names have been distinct from Latin names, to avoid confusion.

Often, as plant breeders have made so many changes, the original species name is not applicable and is dropped completely, as with *Calceolaria* 'Sunshine'.

Names in parentheses, such as the above *Nepeta hederacea*, are synonyms that are in common usage, but are incorrect. Many books and catalogues still use these names, so they are included here for reference. Incorrect botanical names are not cross-referenced in the encyclopedia section, but they are listed in the index, followed by the correct botanical name.

The name shown in double quotation marks is the common name. One plant may have dozens of common names. In most areas of horticulture, growers use only botanical names, but in the bedding plant industry, common names are often used, even in commercial seed catalogues. Catalogues for home gardeners are set out either by botanical name or by common name, so it is best to know both.

The last name, shown in capitals, is the name of the plant family, which includes closely related genera. (It may or may not be capitalized in normal use and is not italicized.) The family name can usually be recognized by the ending *aceae* attached to the stem of the name of a genus within the family. Thus, LAMIACEAE, the name for the mint family, is composed of the stem *Lami*, from the name of a genus in the family, with *aceae* attached. Four old family names, with which you may have been familiar, have changed in accordance with these rules. COMPOSITAE has been changed to ASTERACEAE, CRUCIFERAE to BRASSICACEAE, LABIATAE to LAMIACEAE and LEGUMINOSAE to FABACEAE.

One note regarding ASTERACEAE, the huge family which includes chrysanthemum, marguerite daisy, sunflower and black-eyed susan: what most people think of as the flower is actually made up of many small flowers of two types. The outer "petals" are themselves individual flowers (ray florets), which are open and flattened. The central disk is composed of many tiny flowers (disk florets) pressed closely together. In the text, the familiar term petal is sometimes used to refer to the ray florets; although technically incorrect, it is easier to understand.

All-America Selections and Fleuroselect winners

Two international organizations select outstanding bedding plants. All-America Selections (AAS) has 33 trial grounds in Canada and the United States; judging results from all trial grounds are compiled to determine the winners. Fleuroselect has 22 trial grounds from Finland to southern Italy. Each year, trial ground nurseries receive seed of new plants, which are identified by number only, with no reference to breeder, to discourage prejudice. They also receive seed of the best corresponding bedding plants of each type on the market, for comparison. Old and new are grown side by side and notes on performance are made through the season. Awards are given to those new cultivars which are outstanding. In the Fleuroselect trials, scoring is heavily weighted towards plants that are a breakthrough in breeding, whether or not they are top-notch for the home garden.

Pacific Northwest AAS trial grounds are located at the Department of Plant Science of the University of British Columbia and at Daehnfeldt, Inc., in Albany, Oregon. AAS winners are noted in Canadian and American seed catalogues; Fleuroselect winners are more often seen in British catalogues.

Abutilon hybridum and ***Abutilon pictum*** '**Thompsonii**' (*A. strictum* 'Thompsonii') "flowering maple" MALVACEAE
(Figure 1-1)

Flowering maple is a specialty bedding plant. It is used outdoors in bedding schemes in summer and is often trained as a standard. It must be overwintered in a greenhouse or indoors in a sunny window. A shrub in its native South America, it has maple-shaped leaves and nodding bell-like flowers in shades of white, yellow, orange or red. There are many named cultivars, some of which have variegated foliage. 'Thompsonii' has orange flowers and leaves that are mottled yellow due to the presence of a harmless virus.

Bloomtime: May to October.

Height: 2–4 feet (61–122 cm) in a pot, taller if trained as a standard.

Light and soil: Flowering maples prefer full sun but will tolerate some shade in a warm, sheltered place. Plant in a well-drained soil to which some organic matter has been added.

How to grow: Young plants are sometimes available from shops in spring if you look in the houseplant section. They may also be started from seeds or cuttings. Sow seeds indoors in March or April. Germination, at 60°F (15°C) soil temperature, takes about 20 days. Pinch out the growing tips when about 8 inches (20 cm) high to get a bushy plant, or train the plant as a standard. Refer to directions under *Fuchsia*, but train only one trunk. Set hardened-off plants out in late May, spacing them 18 inches (46 cm) apart. Water freely during spring and summer and give a half-strength liquid fertilizer recommended in Chapter 3 every second week from May to August. In September, bring plants into the greenhouse, or into a cool room indoors, giving them at least four hours of direct sunlight each day. Extra lighting may be required to keep plants bushy.

Pests and diseases: Watch for SCALE, WHITEFLY and MEALY BUGS indoors.

Uses: Grown as a bush, flowering maples are delightful in hanging baskets and window boxes because their flowers are easier to see than if they were planted in the ground. As standards, they are striking as a centerpiece to a formal bedding scheme or a large planter.

Ageratum houstonianum "ageratum" "flossflower" ASTERACEAE
(Figures 5-1 and 7-7)

A half-hardy annual, this native of Central America gets top marks for all-season bloom with a minimum of effort. Ageratum is usually just coming into bloom in packs in late May and continues blooming until the temperature dips below freezing. It prefers warm weather, so don't try to rush the season by planting in April or even early May.

The leaves of ageratum are up to 2 inches (5 cm) across and are roughly triangular in shape. The deep vein pattern and tiny hairs give them a textured appearance. The leaves, however, are almost completely hidden by the small fuzzy flowers which cover the plant.

There are many good cultivars of blue ageratums, but 'Blue Puffs' does particularly well on our coast. 'Royal Delft' tends to burn out. The white cultivars look messy because the flowers become brownish as they fade. There are mixed colors and tall types for cut and dried flowers available from seed companies.

Bloomtime: June to frost.

Height: 6–24 inches (15–61 cm), depending on the cultivar.

Light and soil: Full sun or part shade and a well-drained soil to which some organic matter has been added.

Propagation: Young plants are readily available from shops in spring, or they may be grown from seeds. Sow in late February or early March on the surface of the potting soil and leave the pots uncovered, as light aids in germination. This, at 60–70OF (15–21°C) soil temperature, takes up to 8 days. Grow on at a soil temperature of 60–65°F (15–18°C). Young plants develop slowly.

When the weather has stabilized in late May or early June, set out young plants, spacing dwarf varieties 6–9 inches (15–23 cm) apart, tall types 12 inches (30 cm) apart.

Pests and diseases: Foot and root ROTS sometimes cause plants to collapse at ground level, a good reason not to plant too soon in spring.

Uses: Edging, pattern plantings and planter boxes for dwarf cultivars; border and cutting for taller cultivars.

"Alyssum, sweet" see *Lobularia*

Amaranthus caudatus "love-lies-bleeding" "tasselflower"
Amaranthus hybridus var. *erythrostachys* (*A. hypochondriachus*) "prince's feather"
Amaranthus tricolor "Joseph's coat" AMARANTHACEAE
(Figures 6-1 and 1-2)

Loves-lies-bleeding is an unusual tropical native that has been popular since the 16th century. Although it is not readily available in shops, it is easy to grow from seed. It grows to about 4 feet (1.2 m) and produces striking 18-inch (46-cm) red tassels. Leaves are rounded at the base, taper to a point and are rather coarse. The cultivar 'Viridis' has green tassels and is popular with flower arrangers.

Prince's feather has upright flowers in red ('Pigmy Torch') or green ('Green Thumb') which are excellent cut.

Joseph's coat is noted for its brilliantly colored leaves, but it prefers hotter weather than even our warmest Pacific coast summers provide.

Bloomtime: July to September, looking best in July and August.

Height: Love-lies-bleeding grows to 3–4 feet (.9–1.2 m); prince's feather and Joseph's coat grow to 2 feet (61 cm).

Light and soil: Prefers full sun and any well-drained soil to which some organic matter has been added.

How to grow: Although young plants are not generally available from shops, they are easily grown from seed. In March to April, sow and cover very lightly. Germination, at 60–70°F (15–21°C) soil temperature takes 8–10 days. Grow seedlings on at 70°F (21°C). Set hardened-off plants out in late May, spacing them 18 inches (46 cm) apart. Alternatively, sow seeds in the garden in April, thinning to 18 inches (46 cm) apart in May. Light staking may be required. Joseph's coat should be planted closer together, as it is not as vigorous.

Pests and diseases: APHIDS sometimes infest plants.

Uses: Love-lies-bleeding is an unusual and fascinating annual. It makes an effective dot plant in formal bedding schemes or the center of a large planter. Plant prince's feather for cutting and Joseph's coat for foliage.

"Amethyst flower" see *Browallia*
"Animated oat" see *Avena*

Antirrhinum majus "snapdragon" SCROPHULARIACEAE
(Figure 1-3)

This popular flower from the Mediterranean has fascinated people for centuries and has picked up some interesting names along the way. Its common name, snapdragon, refers to the fact that if the sides of the flowers are pinched, the flower opens and snaps shut. It is also called dog-head, lion-mouth and wolf-muzzle in Greek, Latin and French respectively. In the Middle Ages, however, it was known as the caprice flower, for if a girl wore a spray of snapdragons it meant that she refused her lover's suit. It was also thought that snapdragons possessed magical qualities.

The fragrant blooms are red, bronze, rose, pink, yellow, white and bicolored. The flowers appear atop the stems in spikes, set off by simple bright green leaves.

Breeders have produced many cultivars. The 'Rocket' series is 3 feet (.9 m) tall and perfect for cutting. Dwarf bedding cultivars under 12 inches (30 cm) include 'Kolibri', 'Minaret' and 'Floral Carpet'. Some no longer "snap": 'Madame Butterfly', 24 inches (61 cm), and 'Sweetheart', 12 inches (30 cm), have double flowers that resemble azaleas. 'Bright Butterflies', 30 inches (76 cm), and 'Little Darling', 12 inches (30 cm), have trumpet-shaped blooms. Because of their expanded blooms, these last four show more color than traditional snapdragons. The 1987 AAS winner 'Princess White with a Purple Eye' is a striking bicolor which grows to 14–16 inches (35–40 cm) and does well in our area.

In the wild, snapdragons are perennial and they may survive a mild winter to bloom early the following spring. They are generally grown as half-hardy annuals.

Bloomtime: May or June to frost, if old flowers are removed.

Height: 12–36 inches (30–91 cm), depending on the cultivar.

Light and Soil: Snapdragons bloom best in full sun, but will tolerate light shade. A light, well-drained soil to which lime and organic matter have been added is ideal. They will also tolerate stony soil. Water well during dry spells.

How to grow: Young plants of many cultivars are readily available from shops in spring, or they may be started from seed in February. Pre-chill seeds at 40°F (4°C) for 5 days. Sow, gently pressing the seeds into the surface of the soil, but do not cover, as the seeds need light for germination. Cover the pots or flats with clear glass or plastic to maintain constant humidity. Germination, at 60–70°F (15–21°C) soil temperature, takes about 7 days. When true leaves appear, transplant and lower the temperature to 50°F (10°C), which keeps plants short and compact. Taller cultivars may require pinching. Set the hardened-off plants out in late April, spacing them 9–18 inches (23–46 cm) apart, depending on the cultivar. Pinch the tips when planting, and stake tall cultivars if they are in a windy location. Snapdragons may be planted out earlier than most bedding plants as they will tolerate some cold weather. If plants purchased from shops have flowers on them, pinch them off when planting out. Remove old flower spikes to encourage continued bloom.

Pests and diseases: APHIDS may infest growing tips. In some areas and years, RUST is a serious problem. If it infects your snapdragons, look in seed catalogues for rust-resistant cultivars. If plants show any signs of rust, do not allow them to overwinter; dig them up and put them in the garbage.

Uses: Use at the front, middle or back of the border or mixed bed depending on height. Shorter types are also suitable for container cultivation.

"Aster, China or annual", see *Callistephus*

Avena sterilis "animated oat"
Briza maxima "quaking grass"
Lagurus ovatus "hare's tail" POACEAE

These are only three of a number of hardy annual ornamental grasses which are fun to grow. Although in different genera, they are grouped together here because of their similarity in cultivation and use. They are unusual and attractive in the garden and fresh in flower arrangements. All may be dried to be used in flower arrangements or for decorating wreaths. Animated oat comes from the north coast of Africa and has long "beards" from the seed capsules that twist and turn depending on how much moisture there is in the air. Quaking grass has seed heads that droop from wiry stems and tremble with the slightest breeze. Hare's tail has erect seed heads that are fluffy like a rabbit's tail. The last two species are native to the Mediterranean.

Bloomtime: Seed heads appear in late summer.
Height: Animated oats reach 36 inches (91 cm), quaking grass and hare's tail reach 18 inches (46 cm).
Light and soil: Full sun and well-drained soil.
How to grow: Sow seeds in the garden in April. Germination takes about three weeks. Space plants about 6 inches (15 cm) apart.
Pests and diseases: Generally trouble-free.
Uses: Annual ornamental grasses add movement to the garden and a soft texture to mixed plantings. Throw a few seeds into a mixed planter for contrast. Fresh and dried seed heads are great for arrangements and crafts.

"Baby blue eyes" see *Nemophila*
"Bachelor's button" see *Centaurea*

Begonia x*semperflorens-cultorum* "fibrous begonia" "wax begonia"
BEGONIACEAE
(Figure 2-1)

These simple and delightful bedding plants have a remarkably complex parentage made up of six species of begonias from Central and South America and Jamaica. The name fibrous refers to their roots, to separate them from their cousins, the tuberous begonias, which form a bulb-like tuber.

Fibrous begonias have shiny heart-shaped leaves up to 2 inches (5 cm) across. Leaf color may be bright green or bronze. There are dozens of the small pink, red or white flowers on the plant all season, making a colorful contribution to the garden whether the summer is wet or dry. These begonias are also very easy to grow.

Bloomtime: May to frost. (Pot them up and bring indoors for all-winter bloom.)

Height: 6–9 inches (15–23 cm).

Light and soil: Begonias thrive in sun or shade and any well-drained soil, preferably enriched with moist peat moss or other organic matter.

How to grow: Fibrous begonias are readily available from shops in spring and are very slow to grow from seed, so most gardeners prefer to buy them. If you would like to try growing your own, seeds must be sown in January. The seeds are dust-like, with about 2 million seeds per ounce (28 g). To make sowing easier, mix seeds with a tablespoon (15 mL) of granulated sugar and sow on the surface of the potting mix, pressing it down gently. Do not cover it with soil, as light is required for germination. To maintain humidity, cover flats or pots with clear plastic or glass. Germination, at 70°F (21°C) soil temperature, takes 14–21 days. When seedlings emerge, fertilize with quarter-strength 20-20-20 and maintain soil temperature at 70°F (21°C) until April, then grow at 60°F (15°C). Set hardened-off plants out in late May, spacing them 8 inches (20 cm) apart. Plants may be taken into the house before the frost, where they will bloom all winter, even in a north-facing room. They may be planted out again the following spring. Cuttings can be taken from overwintered plants in spring, which is easier than growing them from seeds.

Pests and diseases: In some years, CUTWORMS may eat stems at ground level. Watch young plants carefully for any sign of damage in the first weeks after planting them out.

Uses: Edging, pattern plantings, rock gardens, planter boxes and the front of flower beds or mixed borders.

Begonia x*tuberhybrida* "tuberous begonia" BEGONIACEAE
(Figure 1-4)

From eight Andean species, begonia hybridizers have developed a dazzling array of flower types in this group. Most popular are the cultivars with double blooms up to 6 inches (15 cm) across in shades of pink, white, rose, red, yellow and orange. (The showy blooms are actually the male flowers; the two smaller female flowers are alongside.) The excellent seed series 'Nonstop' is available in ten separate colors or as a mixture.

Fancy cultivars have ruffled, frilled, picotee and two-toned flowers. These must be grown from tubers, which are available from shops in

March. Leaves, up to 8 inches (20 cm) long, are rounded at the base and taper to a long point. They are dark green and have deep ridges and teeth along the edges, giving them a rich texture. Although they are referred to as tuberous-rooted begonias, a tuber is actually a modified stem rather than a thickened root. Begonia societies offer much specialty information and a chance to purchase unusual begonias.

Often sold as 'Pendula' begonias, hanging basket begonias are part of this group of hybrids. They have smaller flowers and more tapered, pointed leaves. Their trailing habit makes them excellent additions to any type of container.

Bloomtime: May to frost.

Height: 8–18 inches (20–46 cm) depending on the cultivar. The 'Pendula' cultivars have a trailing habit that makes them excellent for hanging baskets.

Light and soil: Tuberous begonias need shade or part shade and a well-drained soil that does not dry out, preferably enriched with moist peat moss.

How to grow: Like fibrous begonias, it is easier for home gardeners to purchase tuberous begonias as tubers or as young plants in spring, rather than to grow them from seed. Both are readily available in shops. Tubers should be planted in March, concave side up, with the top edge level with the soil surface. Use a peaty potting mix, setting the tubers in individual pots or one inch (2.5 cm) apart in a sturdy flat. Do not overwater. Grow indoors in a bright window until hardening off and setting out in late May.

Young plants of cultivars such as 'Nonstop' are available in spring and may be planted out in late May 12–15 inches (30–38 cm) apart. If you wish to try growing them from seed, follow the instructions for fibrous begonias. Tall-growing cultivars may need light staking. In late September or early October, dig the tubers and let the stems dry back. Pack them in a box of dry peat and store in a cool, dry, frost-free place until February or March. Tubers can be kept for over twenty years.

After a year or so, tubers will be large enough to divide if desired. To do this, set tubers out on a bright window sill in March, concave side up (without soil or pots), until the new shoots appear. Divide the tubers with a clean sharp knife, making sure each section has at least one shoot. Dust with a fungicide and plant as with whole tubers.

Pests and diseases: POWDERY MILDEW causes white powdery patches or spots on leaves and stems.

Uses: Bedding, planter boxes and tubs, and hanging baskets. Moss baskets planted with a single cultivar of tuberous begonia are lovely.

"Bells of Ireland" see *Molucella*
"Black-eyed susan" see *Rudbeckia*
"Black-eyed-susan vine" see *Thunbergia*

Brachycome iberidifolia "Swan River daisy" ASTERACEAE
(Figure 2-2)

This half-hardy annual from Australia has ¾-inch (2-cm) daisy-like flowers of pink, violet and white. They are lightly fragrant, although the fragrance is not noticeable unless they are close at hand. The foliage is fine, giving an airy quality to the plant. The plants have a floppy habit, so they need the support of twigs, or they can be grown in containers and allowed to trail. Some seed catalogues list selected strains with more intense color, such as 'Purple Splendor' and 'Blue Splendor'.

Bloomtime: June to September.
Height: Up to 18 inches (46 cm) if staked.
Light and soil: Full sun and rich soil to which some moist peat or well-rotted manure has been added.
How to grow: Although young plants are not generally available from shops, they are easily grown from seed. Sow in March, just covering them with soil. Germinate at 70°F (21°C) until seedlings are established, then transplant and reduce temperature to 60°F (15°C). Set out hardened-off plants in late May, adding small twiggy branches to give support. Pinch the growing tip to encourage bushiness. Plants may be cut back by one-half if they become too floppy.
Pests and diseases: Generally trouble-free.
Uses: Best used in planter boxes and hanging baskets. In the flower border, be sure to support them and plant with other annuals for more impact.

Brassica oleracea "ornamental cabbage" "ornamental kale" "flowering cabbage" "flowering kale" BRASSICACEAE
(Figure 5-2)

Vegetables grown for their decorative rather than nutritive value, these plants have been developed by the Japanese from a European kale. The common name ornamental kale is more accurate than flowering kale, because the decorative part of the plant is the leaves rather than a flower. Color variations include purple, green and white. Some cultivars have tight rosettes of leaves (usually referred to as cabbages) while some have deeply cut feathery leaves (referred to as kale). In a wet winter, the more open plants perform best because the rain can drain away more easily.
Bloomtime: Grown for foliage rather than the flowers. Plants set out in the

autumn give fall and winter color until about March, depending on the winter. As the weather warms, the plants will "bolt," that is, grow taller and begin to flower. The tall yellow flower clusters aren't particularly attractive, and the plants will begin to smell of rotten eggs, so they should be removed as soon as they start to stretch.

Height: 1–2 feet (30–61 cm).

Light and soil: Full sun or light shade. As the plants will not be doing much growing, soil need not be rich as long as it is well-drained.

How to grow: Plants are readily available from shops in the fall, or they may be started from seed sown in July. Transplant seedlings into one-gallon size pots, 6 inches wide by 9 inches deep (15 cm by 23 cm), and fertilize heavily to achieve fast growth. Use full-strength 20-20-20 weekly, stopping when the desired size is achieved or when the weather cools off, mid-September to early October. Set plants out in autumn after summer bedding has been removed. Space them so that they just about touch, and plant them deep, up to the base of the bottom leaves. They will not grow much more during the winter.

Pests and diseases: The CABBAGE BUTTERFLY, white with pale green spots on its wings, will flutter daintily around your cabbage and kale and lay eggs, soon to be followed by hard-to-spot green CATERPILLARS that will rapidly eat all the leaves if not stopped. They often lie along a leaf midrib and are easy to hand pick.

Uses: Fall and winter bedding plants in borders or containers.

Briza see *Avena*

Browallia speciosa and **B. viscosa** "browallia" "amethyst flower"
SOLANACEAE
(Figure 5-3)

Good habit, foliage and flowers make browallia a welcome addition to any planter, hanging basket or border. Its flowers of white, blue or violet have five petals and resemble stars. The simple, bright green leaves taper to a point at each end. Most cultivars are well-branched and bushy. This South American native is a half-hardy perennial and will continue blooming in a greenhouse or sunny window indoors in winter. It doesn't like cold weather, so you probably won't see it in shops in April or early May, but it is worth waiting for.

'Sapphire' is deep blue, 'Heavenly Bells' is light Cambridge blue, 'Marine Bells' is indigo, 'Silver Bells' is white and 'Jingle Bells' is a mixture. All are bushy and compact.

Bloomtime: June to first cold weather, September or October.
Height: 10–12 inches (25–30cm).
Light and soil: Sun or partial shade and a well-drained soil. Add organic matter if possible, but browallia tolerates even poor, dry soil.
How to grow: Young plants are generally available from shops in late spring, or they may be started from seed. Sow indoors in March, but do not cover, as light is required for germination. Germination, at 70°F (21°C) soil temperature, takes about 14 days. After transplanting, grow on at 60°F (15°C). When weather has warmed up in late May or early June, set out young plants 8–10 inches (20–25 cm) apart. Pinch growing tips to encourage branching.
Pests and diseases: Watch for WHITEFLY under leaves.
Uses: Edging, pattern plantings and at the front of beds and mixed borders. Excellent in containers and hanging baskets. Try blue browallia with yellow dwarf French marigolds; white browallia with peach tuberous begonias looks quite elegant.

"Burning bush" see *Kochia*
"Butterfly flower" see *Schizanthus*
"Cabbage, flowering or ornamental" see *Brassica*
"Cabbage tree" see *Cordyline*

Calceolaria **'Sunshine'** "pocketbook flower" "slipper flower" "pouch flower" "calceolaria" SCROPHULARIACEAE
(Figures 7-1 and 8-6)
 Many calceolaria are sold in florists' shops for indoor decoration, but 'Sunshine' is the best one to grow in the garden. ('Goldri' is also excellent and very similar, but it is not readily available.) 'Sunshine' is a hybrid of *Calceolaria integrifolia* (formerly *C. rugosa*) and an unknown parent. It has a most unusual yellow flower, which is shaped like a pouch. Its leaves are mat green, crinkled and tapering to a point. A subshrub in its native Chile, calceolaria is grown as a half-hardy annual in the Pacific coastal region.
Bloomtime: May or June to September.
Height: 8–10 inches (20–25 cm).
Light and soil: Full sun or part shade and a well-drained soil. They like a warm spot protected from the wind.
How to grow: Young plants are sometimes available from shops in spring, or they may be started from seed. Sow seeds indoors in March, but do not cover as light is required for germination, which, at 70°F (21°C) soil temperature, takes about 14–16 days. After transplanting, grow on at 50–55°F

(10–13°C). Set hardened-off plants out in late May, spacing them 8 inches (20 cm) apart. Plants dug up at the end of the season can be overwintered in a bright, cool, frost-free place.

Pests and diseases: In the garden, SLUGS and APHIDS may bother these plants. In the greenhouse they may get WHITEFLY and root or basal ROTS.

Uses: For edging and the front of beds and borders. *Calceolaria* 'Sunshine' also makes an outstanding moss basket or may be added to a mixed basket.

Calendula officinalis "English marigold" "pot marigold" ASTERACEAE (Figure 8-1)

This easy-to-grow hardy annual was the "marigold" of the Elizabethans, who used it for cooking and decorating food. The specific name *officinalis* indicates that it was used by apothecaries for medicinal purposes. The wild species, native to southern Europe, grows up to 2 feet (61 cm) tall and has single daisy-like blooms of yellow or orange. Plant breeders have developed strains with double blooms in the same color range with the addition of apricot. 'Fiesta Gitana' (a Fleuroselect winner) and 'Bon Bon' grow to 12 inches (30 cm); 'Pacific Beauty', 18–24 inches (46–61 cm). 'Apricot Sherbet' is a lovely peach shade and grows to 15 inches (38 cm). While pot marigolds thrive even in poor soil with neglect, they will have more fully double blooms and bloom for a longer period if the soil is better and old flowers are removed. If flowers go to seed or if the weather is exceptionally hot, plants tend to look untidy by late July. Calendula will reseed itself, which is a blessing or a nuisance, depending on the plant's location and your point of view. It is easy to start another crop in June for flowers in the fall, if desired. Calendula is an excellent cut flower, particularly the taller varieties.

Bloomtime: May to late summer, fall for a second crop.

Height: 12–24 inches (30–61 cm) depending on the cultivar.

Light and soil: Prefer full sun and any well-drained soil. They will tolerate amazingly dry and poor soil, but may not bloom as heavily or have as many double blooms.

How to grow: Young plants are generally available from shops in spring, or they may be started easily from seed. Sow seeds indoors in March and cover lightly as seeds germinate best in darkness. Germination, at 60°F (15°C) soil temperature, takes about 10 days. After transplanting, grow on at 50°F (10°C). Set young plants out in April, pinching growing tips to encourage bushiness.

Pests and diseases: Pot marigolds are generally not bothered by problems, but POWDERY MILDEW may cause white powder on leaves if spring weather is cool. Watch for APHIDS; CUTWORMS may eat stems.

Uses: Use dwarf cultivars at the front of beds and the taller ones in mixed borders for a "cottage garden look." Good for cutting.

"Calliopsis" see *Coreopsis*

Callistephus chinensis "China aster" "annual aster" ASTERACEAE
(Figure 3-1)

In the 1730s, a Jesuit priest in China first sent seeds of a dark purple half-hardy annual to Europe. Although his name has been forgotten, his contribution to western horticulture has not. That original species had single flowers and was thought to be in the same genus as the perennial aster (*Aster*). More recently it has been appointed its own genus, *Callistephus*, meaning beautiful crown. Over the years, many colors have been developed from this one species, including red, pink, blue, violet, white, pale yellow and bicolors. Breeders have produced a dazzling array of flower forms—some like pompons, some with long needle-like petals, some like daisies and some with large, shaggy blooms. Unfortunately, China asters don't bloom until August or September, and they are prone to the serious disease aster wilt, which may kill plants completely. But do try a few, especially in an out-of-the-way corner of the garden where problems might go unnoticed if they develop. Even one row of asters will give dozens of stunning cut flowers.

Plant hybridizers have developed a number of seed strains that have increased resistance to aster wilt. 'Dwarf Queen' reaches 8 inches (20 cm) and is covered with double 2½" (6 cm) blooms of red, scarlet, light blue, rose pink, white, yellow and mixed colors. 'Pompon Mixed' reaches 20 inches (51 cm) as tall, upright, well-branched bushes with very tight button-like blooms 2 inches (5 cm) across; the whole plant may be cut at once as a long-lasting bouquet. 'Powderpuff' grows to 36 inches (91 cm) tall and only 12 inches (30 cm) wide; they are very upright plants with blooms 2½ inches (6 cm) across. The whole plant may be cut at once. 'Giant Princess Mixed' has crested centers and quill-like guard petals in a range of 17 different colors and grows to 30 inches (76 cm). 'Ostrich Plume' has recurved petals on double flowers in a wide range of colors, grows to 18 inches (46 cm) and is among the first to bloom.

Bloomtime: Late summer and autumn.

Height: 10–36 inches (25–76 cm), depending on the cultivar.

Light: Full sun and any well-drained soil to which some lime has been added.

How to grow: Young plants are generally available from shops in late spring or early summer. They may also be started from seed sown indoors in April. Cover seeds lightly. Germination, at 60–70°F (15–21°C) soil temperature, takes 8–10 days. Later sowings will extend the season of bloom. Set hardened-off plants out in early June, spacing them 12 inches (30 cm) apart. Seeds may also be sown directly into the garden in April or May. Stake tall cultivars for straighter stems if desired. Insects spread diseases, so keep plants insect-free.

Pests and diseases: ASTER WILT may attack plants. APHIDS may infest plants, transmitting disease from one to another.

Uses: For an excellent cut flower and beautiful late-summer color, try some asters. But don't plant them as the focal point of your garden, because they can be unreliable.

Campanula isophylla "star-of-Bethlehem" CAMPANULACEAE

Although sold in shops in spring, star-of-Bethlehem is a tricky plant to grow outdoors. It is daylength-sensitive and does not bloom until August and September. Plants that are in bloom in May have been forced under lights. The stems are brittle and break easily and the flowers turn brown and yet do not fall off the plant. They are not a good choice for summer bedding; they are more suitable perhaps to bloom in pots in the greenhouse or hanging baskets which can be attended to frequently.

"Candytuft" see *Iberis*

Canna x*generalis* "canna lily" CANNACEAE
(Figure 1-5)

This group of hybrids brings the exotic look of tropical America to the home garden with very little effort. Canna lilies have huge leaves with rounded tips that vary in color from light to dark green, and from brownish to dark red. The flowers, which are up to 4 inches (10 cm) across, grow in spectacular clusters at the top of stems. Depending on the cultivar, they are yellow, orange, red, cream, salmon, or rose, and some are variegated and speckled with two colors. Canna lilies are usually used as a centerpiece in large planters or beds, surrounded by other bedding plants. Use smaller canna cultivars in scale with a home garden. Because cannas form rhizomes (thickened underground stems), they may be dug before the first frost and kept over winter for next year. Look for them with bulbs, rather than with the annuals, in shops and catalogues.

'Seven Dwarfs Mixed' is a seed strain of cannas that grows to only 18 inches (46 cm) high, which is more in scale with a small garden than are some of the taller types. 'Pfitzer's' named cultivars may be purchased as rhizomes; they grow up to 30 inches (76 cm). The giant canna with bronze leaves and red flowers seen in parks is usually 'Red King Humbert', which reaches 7 feet (2.1 m) in height–not for the small garden!

Bloomtime: July to frost.

Height: 1½–7 feet (.5–2.1 m), depending on the cultivar.

Light and soil: Plant in full sun. Canna lilies thrive in a rich moist soil. Add lots of well-decomposed organic matter or moist peat. In the wild, they grow in swampy areas, so they like lots of water.

How to grow: Buy rhizomes of named cultivars and start them indoors in March, barely covered with soil. Fertilize with 20-20-20 and grow on at 60°F (15°C) until planting out in late May. Rhizomes may be set directly in the garden in late May, but will take longer to bloom. In subsequent years, old rhizomes may be divided when new shoots appear, taking care to leave one shoot on each section of rhizome.

Cannas are also easily grown from seed, but may not bloom the first year. Start them in January or February by soaking the seeds in warm water for 24 hours, or nick the seed coats with a file before sowing. Keep the soil temperature at 70°F (21°C). Germination may take several months. When roots of the young plants are filling the pots, pot on into individual containers.

In the garden, remove faded flowers constantly. In late October cut the stems back to 6–8 inches (15–20 cm) and dig the rhizomes. Shake off the soil, partially dry them and store in a cool, frost-free place in a box of dry peat. Check for signs of shriveling (sprinkle with water) or rot (remove affected rhizomes).

Pests and diseases: SLUGS and CUTWORMS may eat the rhizomes.

Uses: For a touch of the exotic, plant cannas at the back or center of beds or the center of large planters.

"Carnation" see *Dianthus*

Catananche caerulea "cupid's dart" ASTERACEAE
(Figure 5-4)
    A hardy perennial from the Mediterranean, cupid's dart is included here

because it blooms the first year from seed and continues all summer. It has attractive, narrow, gray-green leaves and blue flowers with papery petals, similar to a cornflower. They are good as fresh and dry cut flowers.

Bloomtime: June to October.

Height: 18–30 inches (46–91 cm).

Light and soil: Full sun or part shade and any well-drained garden soil to which some organic matter has been added.

How to grow: Plants may be found in the perennials section of your garden shop, or start seeds indoors in March. Germinate at 55–60°F (13–15°C), transplant, harden off and set outdoors in May, spaced 15 to 18 inches (38 to 46 cm) apart. Do not remove in fall, as they are hardy perennials.

Pests and diseases: Generally trouble-free.

Uses: Great in a mixed border for an old-fashioned look. Good for cutting and drying.

Catharanthus roseus (*Vinca rosea*) "Madagascar periwinkle" APOCYNACEAE

Listed in many books as heat tolerant, the problem with the Madagascar periwinkle is that it doesn't tolerate cool weather. In a wet spring, plants will turn yellow and die suddenly. It is not usually worth growing in Pacific coast areas.

Celosia cristata "celosia" "cockscomb" AMARANTHACEAE

(Figure 1-6)

Cultivars of this striking half-hardy annual fall into two groups: flowers in the Plumosa Group are fluffy and feathery, while those in the Crested Group are dense and sculpted, somewhat resembling a cock's comb. The flowers, in shades of red, orange, yellow, pink and cream, seem to glow. Leaves are up to 4 inches (10 cm) long and taper to a point at each end. The Plumosa cultivars are most successful in Pacific coast gardens. 'New Look' has bronze foliage and scarlet plumes on 12-inch (30-cm) plants. 'Apricot Brandy' has golden plumes set off by brandy-colored leaves. An AAS winner in 1985, 'Century Mixed' grows to 28 inches (71 cm) in a wide selection of colors. Celosia is native to the tropics of Asia and does best in a warm, dry summer.

Bloomtime: June to frost. Purchased in shops, celosia generally have one large plume that will last all season with a few smaller plumes developing on side shoots. If the central flower is pinched out when planting, a bushier plant will develop with many very small plumes. If, however, celosia can be planted "green," that is, before plants begin to bloom, the maximum number of blooms will result. This is an advantage of growing them from seed yourself.

Height: 10–24 inches (25–61 cm) depending on the cultivar. Plant taller ones for good cut flowers.

Light and soil: Full sun and rich, well-drained soil are ideal, but celosia will also tolerate poor, dry soil.

How to grow: Young plants are generally available from shops in spring, or they can be grown easily from seed. Sow in April and cover seeds very lightly to prevent them from drying out. Germination, at 70°F (21°C) soil temperature, takes about 14 days. Continue growing plants at the same temperature after transplanting. Harden off in late May and plant outdoors in early June. Space 8–12 inches (20–30 cm) apart. (They don't grow a lot in width, so plant dwarf cultivars closer together, especially in poor soils.)

Pests and diseases: Root ROT may occur if soil is too cold or damp.

Uses: Edging, bedding and pattern plantings; containers; cut and dried flowers. Some gardeners find cockscomb too gaudy; some like their festive colors.

Centaurea cyanus "cornflower" "bachelor's button" ASTERACEAE
(Figure 5-5)

Loved since ancient times, cornflower was named *cyanus* by the Romans in honor of its heavenly blue color. In Britain and Europe, this hardy annual grows wild with red field poppies (*Papaver rhoeas*) in wheat fields. Because the British refer to wheat as corn, these flowers were called cornflowers. Growing to 30 inches (76 cm), cornflowers are slender and airy, with long narrow leaves and 1- to 2-inch (2.5- to 5-cm) flowers with many ragged petals. 'Blue Diadem' has fully double flowers 2½ inches (6 cm) across; 'Polka Dot Mixed' grows to a bushy 16 inches (41 cm) and blooms in shades of blue, maroon, red, rose-pink, lavender and white.

Bloomtime: If deadheaded constantly, cornflowers will bloom all summer. Otherwise, they tend to stop flowering, although self-sown seedlings grow quickly and often bloom the same season.

Height: 16–30 inches (41–76 cm), depending on the cultivar

Light and soil: Plants are healthiest in a spot with good air circulation and full sun. Any soil is satisfactory.

How to grow: Although young plants are not generally available from shops, they are easily grown from seed. Sow seeds directly in the garden, ½ inch (1 cm) deep, in September, March or April; plants will bloom early in the spring from a fall or early spring sowing. Thin seedlings to stand 6–10 inches (15–25 cm) apart. Sow at several different times to extend the season of bloom. If sown indoors in March, use individual pots, as corn-flowers resent transplanting. No bottom heat is required. Harden off plants and set out in early May. Staking of tall varieties is not always necessary as stems are wiry and quite strong.

Pests and diseases: Cornflowers are vulnerable to POWDERY MILDEW, which causes white fuzzy patches on the foliage. Plant in full sun with good air circulation and avoid overhead watering.

Uses: Because they have a softening effect, both in texture and color, corn-flowers do not look out of place in an "English country" style of gar-den. They make excellent cut flowers and may be grown in the middle of a mixed border.

Cheiranthus cheiri "English wallflower"
Erysimum hieraciifolium (*Cheiranthus allioni*) "Siberian wallflower"
BRASSICACEAE
(Figure 7-4)

Although these two wallflowers are now assigned to separate genera, they are grouped together here because of their similar appearance, cultiva-tion and use in the garden. Both are perennials grown as winter annuals, blooming very early in the spring. They are excellent planted with tulips and for early color until warm-weather bedding plants can be set out. Fra-grant flower spikes of gold, yellow, cream, bronze or rich red are set off by slender green leaves. Both species are native to Europe.

Bloomtime: English wallflowers, April to June; Siberian wallflowers, May to July.

Height: 9–24 inches (23–61 cm), depending on the cultivar.

Light and soil: Full sun or part shade in well-drained soil with a neutral or slightly sweet pH.

How to grow: Plants are sometimes available in shops in spring or you may grow them from seed. Sow in an open nursery bed in May or June (or in the vegetable garden after the early peas have come out). Thin or transplant to 8 inches (20 cm) apart. When they are 6 inches (15 cm) tall, pinch out the growing tips so they will become bushy. In September to November, move the plants to where they are to bloom. (Winter pansies like the same routine, so they can be done at the same time.) If you wish, leave wallflowers in the garden to naturalize in a wild corner with good sun. They will bloom every spring.

Pests and diseases: Generally trouble-free.

Uses: Plants add green to the winter garden. Use for spring bedding with flowering bulbs such as tulips and daffodils. Use dwarf cultivars for rock gardens and niches on a rock wall, tall ones for cutting.

"Cherry pie" see *Heliotropium*
"China pink" see *Dianthus*

Chrysanthemum carinatum (*C. tricolor*) "annual chrysanthemum"
ASTERACEAE
(Figure 8-2)

Annual chrysanthemum is a hardy annual from North Africa. It grows quickly, making a 2-foot (61-cm) bush that is covered in blooms by late June from a May planting. The daisy-like flowers are 2½ inches (6 cm) across, the petals having concentric rings of white, yellow, red and bronze. They are set off by the finely cut, bright green, almost succulent foliage. Handsome in the garden, they are a long-lasting cut flower as well.

Bloomtime: June to September, looking best in July and August.

Height: 18–24 inches (46–61 cm).

Light and soil: Best in full sun in a rich, well-drained soil.

How to grow: Although young plants are not generally available from shops, they are easily grown from seed. Sow directly in the garden or indoors in late March. No bottom heat is required. Set out young plants or thin seedlings to 12 inches (30 cm) apart. Give light support with bamboo stakes. Pinch the tips to encourage more side shoots. Remove old flowers to extend the season of bloom and then keep well-watered or the plants will flag in hot weather.

Pests and diseases: Generally trouble-free.

Uses: A fast filler for mid-summer color, annual chrysanthemums make good cut flowers also. Use in the middle of a mixed border.

Chrysanthemum frutescens "marguerite daisy" ASTERACEAE
(Figures 6-2 and 7-7)

Marguerites are the troupers of the bedding plant set, blooming tirelessly with little care until frost. In their Canary Island home they are perennials, but here they are grown as annuals in the garden. The most common marguerite has yellow or white daisy flowers up to 2 inches (5 cm) across; both colors have a yellow center. They make excellent cut flowers. There are several fancy cultivars on the market. 'Silver Lace' is a charming cultivar which is very bushy and compact, and has thread-like gray-green foliage. Smothered with 1-inch (2.5-cm) white daisies, it is delightful for any border or large planter, or in small bouquets. 'June Bride' has enlarged, shaggy looking disk florets (anemone-flowered). There is also a single pink that has a lovely flower but is a tall and slightly floppy plant, needing light staking.

Bloomtime: Starts blooming late May and looks great right up to the frost.
Height: 18–24 inches (46–61 cm), depending on the cultivar.
Light and soil: Full sun. Rich, well-drained soil that does not dry out gives the best looking plants.
How to grow: Young plants of many cultivars are readily available from shops in spring, or they may be started from cuttings taken in September. Take 2- to 3-inch (5- to 7.5-cm) cuttings of non-flowering side-shoots and overwinter indoors under lights. Cuttings may also be taken of over-wintered plants in February, but fall cuttings will make larger plants. Set plants out in May. Removal of old flowers makes the plant tidier, but plants will bloom well even if not deadheaded.
Pests and diseases: Generally trouble-free.
Uses: Middle or back of beds and borders; large planters; cut flowers.

Chrysanthemum parthenium "feverfew" "matricaria" ASTERACEAE
(Figure 7-2)
   Feverfew is technically a perennial, but it is short-lived and comes so quickly from seed that it is usually treated as an annual. The deeply cut, bright green leaves are soft and aromatic. Many delightful cultivars have been developed from the original species. 'Aureum' is primarily grown for its golden foliage; 'Golden Ball', 10 inches (25 cm) tall, has clusters of yellow pompons; 'White Bonnet', at 30 inches (76 cm), is fine for cutting. A new cultivar, 'Santana', is said to bloom all summer. Look for feverfew in the perennial section or grow it easily from seed. Although matricaria is not a correct common name, seed is offered under that name in some catalogues. Feverfew is native to Europe.
Bloomtime: On and off throughout the summer until fall. Although each plant blooms for only a month or so, feverfew seeds itself. In a group of plants, new plants will provide fresh flowers through the season. Old plants may be cut out after blooming to make room for new ones.
Height: It forms stiff bushes 6–18 inches (15–46 cm) in height depending on the cultivar.
Light and soil: Full sun is best, average soil.
How to grow: Although young plants are not generally available from shops, they are easily grown from seed. Sow seeds indoors in March or directly in the garden in April. Space 9 inches (23 cm) apart for dwarf

cultivars; 18 inches (46 cm) for taller ones. Feverfew seeds itself. Young plants will provide fresh flowers through the season.

Pests and diseases: POWDERY MILDEW may be a problem.

Uses: Beds and borders, planters and pattern plantings (especially short cultivars); taller cultivars add airiness to bouquets; use them to set off roses and other larger flowers.

Chrysanthemum ptarmiciflorum see *Senecio*
"Cigar flower" see *Cuphea*

Clarkia amoena (*Godetia grandiflora*) "godetia" "satin flower"
ONAGRACEAE
(Figure 4-1)

This charmer, native to this area, was named to commemorate Captain William Clark of the Lewis and Clark expedition of 1804–1806. Even in patches of flowers in the wild, no two flowers are identical. Each flower has four satiny petals in shades of lavender, pink, red, white or rose, with contrasting spots and edging on the petals. The leaves are oblong, up to 2 inches (5 cm) long; the flower buds and seed capsules are held erect at the ends of the stems.

Bloomtime: June to August. Bloomtime may be extended into fall by making later sowings.

Height: 12–24 inches (30–61 cm), depending on the cultivar.

Light and Soil: A light moist soil and full sun give the most blooms. Do not use too much fertilizer.

How to grow: Although young plants are not generally available from shops, they are easily grown from seed. A hardy annual, godetia may be seeded in the garden ¼ inch (.6 cm) deep, in March or April (or start seeds indoors in March). To extend season of bloom, sow again in April and May. Space young plants 12 inches (30 cm) apart. Provide light support for tall cultivars or let them spread and make a clump; they look fine either way. Save seed capsules in August if you want to sow your own seeds.

Pests and diseases: Godetia are generally trouble-free, but APHIDS may appear in early spring and plants may be vulnerable to root ROT if drainage is poor.

Uses: Very showy in a border and long-lasting cut flowers.

Cleome hasslerana "cleome" "spider flower" CAPPARACEAE
(Figure 2-3)

Cleome (clee-oh-mee), an annual from Brazil and Argentina, likes warm weather, so it takes a while to get going, but it makes a striking plant. Growing to a large bush, it has 5-inch (13-cm) leaves divided into 5 to 7 pointed leaflets. At the top of each flower stem is a cluster of flowers, each having four long petals and six 2-inch (5-cm) stamens (the thin flower part which produces the pollen). The flowers farther down the stem develop long, narrow seed pods, which sit out from the stem on wiry stalks. Altogether, it is very unusual. Seed is available, both for separate colors—white ('Helen Campbell'), pink ('Rose Queen'), or violet ('Purple Queen')—and in mixed colors.

Bloomtime: July to frost.

Height: 3–4 feet (.9–1.2 cm) if grown in rich soil.

Light and soil: Full sun is essential. Cleome should be encouraged to grow quickly. Add organic matter to the soil and an all-purpose fertilizer. Soil should be well drained but not dry.

How to grow: Young plants are sometimes available from shops in spring, or they may be started from seed indoors in March. Pot into individual pots when large enough to handle and water weekly with a solution of 20-20-20. Harden off and set out in late May, June in a cold spring, spacing them 18 inches (46 cm) apart. Pinch the growing tips to encourage bushiness. The foliage of cleome has a strong odor, so plants should be set at the back of a bed where they won't be touched. Fertilize throughout the season.

Pests and diseases: CUTWORMS may eat the stem at the soil line. Watch carefully for damage after planting out. APHIDS may infest new growths.

Uses: Background planting at the back of a flower bed or mixed border; centerpiece to a large formal bed.

Cleretum bellidiformis (*Dorotheanthus bellidiformis, Mesembryanthemum criniflorum*) "Livingstone daisy" AIZOACEAE
(Figure 3-2 and front cover)

Livingstone daisy is an annual from South Africa and is named for the famous African explorer, Dr. Livingstone. The narrow, tapering, spoon-shaped leaves are succulent and covered with a glistening coating that gives them a sugar-coated look. Flower colors include white, yellow, orange, pink, and shades of red to purplish-red, often with a contrasting white ring at the center of the flower. The flowers are daisy-like, but they are not true daisies (ASTERACEAE). Flowers close on rainy days. Although grown as a half-hardy annual, plants are quite hardy if kept dry in winter. The name *Cleretum bellidiformis* has recently been given to this species.

Bloomtime: June to August.

Height: 2 inches high by 12 inches across (5 cm by 30 cm).

Light and soil: Full sun and well-drained soil. Tolerates dry soil and likes hot places.

How to grow: Young plants are generally available from shops in spring, or they can be grown from seed. Sow in early March and cover seeds lightly, as darkness aids germination. At 60–70°F (15–21°C), this takes about 14 days. Set hardened-off plants out in late May, spaced 8 inches (20 cm) apart. They may also be sown directly in the garden in April.

Pests and diseases: If the ground is too wet, plants may collapse due to foot ROT. SLUGS will eat the leaves.

Uses: Excellent for color in a rock garden or a hot, sunny corner.

"Cockscomb" see *Celosia*

Coleus x*hybridus* "coleus" LAMIACEAE
(Figure 2-4)

The exotic leaf shapes and colors of coleus can add interest to a shady corner. There have been over 200 named cultivars developed from the Javan parent, *Coleus blumei*. The leaf color range includes red, orange, yellow, cream, bronze and every possible shade of green. Most cultivars have two or three colors on each leaf, with interesting borders and markings. Leaves are velvety and taper to a point, but some cultivars have added ruffles and frills. Although grown as annuals here, coleus are really perennials, and therefore make excellent houseplants in a sunny location. The 'Wizard' series is better in the garden than the 'Carefree' series. The 'Saber' series has very long leaves.

Bloomtime: Flowers should be pinched out before they develop. You will notice them as long spikes that start at the end of the stems. Pinch them off to keep the plant bushy.

Height: 6–18 inches (15–46 cm), depending on the cultivar.

Light and soil: Leaf color is best if plants have bright light, but not hot afternoon sun. Plant in light shade or on the east side of the house. Coleus like a moist, well-drained soil with some organic matter.

How to grow: Young plants are readily available from shops in spring, or they may be started from seed sown indoors in March. Sow at any time of year for houseplants. Do not cover seeds with potting mixture, but cover flats with clear plastic, to maintain humidity, until the seeds have germinated. Germination, at 60–70°F (15–21°C) takes 12–14 days. After transplanting, apply a fungicide drench to control damping-off. Cuttings may be taken in summer from favorite plants and rooted in water or vermiculite. Set young plants 8–12 inches (20–30 cm) apart and pinch out the growing tips to encourage bushiness.

Pests and diseases: Seedlings may DAMP OFF. In the garden, coleus is generally trouble-free.

Uses: An interesting addition to a shady container or corner of the garden. Try adding coleus to a planter with orange tuberous begonias or growing it with the cigar flower in a tub. Coleus also looks handsome in a brick planter in the shade.

Cordyline australis "dracaena palm" "cabbage tree"AGAVACEAE
(Figure 6-3)

A New Zealand native that doesn't normally bloom outdoors in this area, dracaena palm is grown for the decorative effect of the ½-inch-wide (1-cm) leaves, which arch to 3 feet (.9 m) long. Dracaena contrasts well with other bedding plants, and it makes a striking centerpiece for a bed or planter. If you can't find it in the bedding plant section (a strong possibility), look in the houseplant section.

Bloomtime: Grown for its foliage rather than its flowers.

Height: In a container, 3–4 feet (.9–1.3 m).

Light and soil: Full sun or part shade in a fertile, well-drained soil. Dracaenas are drought-resistant and tolerate seaside winds.

How to grow: Young plants are generally available from shops in spring, or they can easily be grown from seed, although they take a year to reach a good size. They are good houseplants and can be grown in the house until they're large enough to make an impact in a planter outdoors. Germination at 70°F (21°C) takes about 2 months. Do not cover the seeds, but press them firmly into the soil surface.

They may also be propagated by removing leaves from mature stems and cutting the stems into 2- to 4-inch (5- to 10-cm) pieces. Place stems vertically in a sand and peat mixture, just buried, on bottom heat. Each eye on the stem will develop a shoot with about six leaves. When top growth appears, pot cutting individually into a 4-inch (10-cm) pot. Grow them in a sunny window indoors.

Plant out dracaenas in late May and bring them back indoors before the first frost. Check under the leaves for insect pests—you may need a magnifying glass to see spider mites. Alternatively, leave plants outdoors, where they will survive a mild winter.

Pests and diseases: SPIDER MITES sometimes infest the underside of the leaves.

Uses: As a centerpiece to a formal bed or planter.

Coreopsis tinctoria "calliopsis" "tickseed" ASTERACEAE
(Figure 1-7)

In 1737, Linnaeus gave the name *Coreopsis* to this genus because its seed resembled lice–from the Greek *koris* (lice) and *opsis* (similarity). Later there was a movement to change it to *Calliopsis*, that is, "beautiful to see" and although this generic name was never formally adopted, it is often used as a common name for the annual species of the genus.

An extremely easy, hardy annual to grow, calliopsis has wiry stems bearing yellow daisies with red and maroon markings. It is native to North America. *Coreopsis* 'Sunray' won a Fleuroselect medal.

Bloomtime: July to frost, if old flowers are removed, an onerous task, as the flowers are small and numerous. If they stop blooming, cut the plants back by one-third for a second bloom.

Height: 9–36 inches (23–91 cm), depending on the cultivar.

Light and soil: Full sun, a light well-drained soil (do not add too much organic matter).

How to grow: Although young plants are not generally available from shops, they are easily grown from seed sown directly in the garden or indoors in March. Space 6–9 inches (15–23 cm) apart. Stake tall cultivars with twiggy branches or bamboo canes.

Pests and diseases: Generally trouble-free.

Uses: Beds and borders; tall cultivars for cutting; dwarfs in mixed containers.

"Cornflower" see *Centaurea*

Cosmos bipinnatus "cosmos"
Cosmos sulphureus "yellow cosmos" ASTERACEAE
(Figure 4-2)

Cosmos and yellow cosmos are half-hardy annuals from Mexico bearing daisy-like flowers. They are not early bloomers, but are outstanding in late summer and fall when many bedding plants look tired. **Cosmos** forms a large bushy plant with feathery, bright green foliage and flowers up to 4 inches (10 cm) across in shades of white, pink, rose or purple-red. The best known cultivar is 'Sensation Mixed', which makes excellent cut flowers. The cultivar 'Sea Shells' has petals rolled like fluted sea shells.

Yellow cosmos is smaller-growing and has darker green, less finely cut foliage. Flower colors include the yellows, orange-reds and flame colors. Look for 'Bright Lights Mixed', 'Diablo' and 'Sunny Red', a 1986 AAS winner.

Bloomtime: August to frost.

Height: Cosmos, to 3–4 feet (.9–1.2 m), depending on the cultivar. Yellow cosmos, to 2–3 feet (.6–.9 m), with some dwarf types 18 inches (46 cm) high.

Light and soil: Blooms best in full sun with light soil that is not too rich. Add moist peat but no fertilizer. Give plenty of water.

How to grow: Easy to grow. Young plants are generally available from shops in spring, or they may be started from seed sown indoors in March. Germination, at 60–70°F (15–21°C) soil temperature, takes about 7 days. Plant out hardened-off plants in late May, spacing 12–18 inches (30–46 cm) apart. Pinch the growing tip to encourage bushiness and, in windy locations, stake plants. Remove faded flowers to encourage blooming.

Pests and diseases: APHIDS may infest young plants.

Uses: Cosmos have a soft effect in the garden and may be used in a mixed border to add texture and color. Plant near perennials such as bleeding heart and oriental poppies that die back in late summer; the cosmos will fill in the spaces. They are also excellent for cutting.

"Cupflower" see *Nierembergia*

Cuphea ignea "cigar flower" "firecracker plant" LYTHRACEAE
(Figure 1-8)

A shrub in its native Mexico and Jamaica, cigar flower makes a delightful annual in Pacific coast gardens and may overwinter outdoors in a mild winter. Bushy and compact, cigar flower has dark green 1½-inch (4-cm) leaves that taper to a point at each end. It bears dozens of ¾-inch (2-cm) orange tubes with white and purple markings at the tip, which do resemble tiny cigars. It is not as showy as some bedding plants (that might be considered an advantage by some gardeners), but is so easy to grow that it should be grown more.

Bloomtime: June to frost.

Height: 12 inches (30 cm).

Light and soil: It is happy in sun or shade, but prefers a rich, well-drained soil that does not dry out.

How to grow: Although young plants are not generally available from shops, they are easily grown from seed sown indoors in mid-February. Germination, at 60–70°F (15–21°C) soil temperature, takes about 14–21 days. Set hardened-off plants out in late May, spacing them 12 inches

(30 cm) apart. After checking for spider mites, plants may be brought indoors for the winter and set on a sunny window sill.

Pests and diseases: Cigar flower may get SPIDER MITES, especially in the greenhouse or indoors.

Uses: Containers, either alone or with other plants (such as dwarf marigolds, white or blue browallia); side planted in moss baskets; edging in beds or borders.

"Cupid's dart" see *Catananche*

Dahlia **hybrids** "dahlia" ASTERACEAE
(Figure 4-3)

There are thousands of dahlia cultivars, and there seem to be almost as many stories about who discovered them in Mexico and how they were brought to Europe. They were certainly being grown in Europe by the early 1800s, and a dahlia craze was launched. In 1826, there were 62 cultivars in England; by 1841 the number had jumped to 1,200. In 1864 the Caledonian Horticultural Society offered a prize of 50,000 francs for anyone who could produce a blue dahlia. The money has yet to be claimed.

The universal popularity of dahlias can be attributed to the ease with which they are grown and the vast array of sizes, shapes and colors available (all except blue!). The leaves are variable in shape, but are generally divided into three leaflets with small teeth and pointed tips.

Only a dozen or so dahlia cultivars are sold as bedding plants. These bloom quickly from seed and are a dwarf 12–15 inches (30–38 cm). Flowers are single, semi-double or double and come in yellow, red, orange, pink or white. Most cultivars are sold as color mixtures, but those in the 'Sunny' series are sold as separate colors and are fully double. 'Redskin' (a Fleuroselect winner) has bronze foliage that sets off the bright double blooms. Seed is available for the "cactus" and "ball" type flowers as well, but these do not bloom as quickly as the bedding types.

Most fancy dahlias are named cultivars and consequently must be propagated by tuber division. Look for named cultivars with the summer-flowering bulbs in shops in March, or mail-order them from a specialist. Although only bedding dahlias are covered in detail here, the fancy dahlias can certainly be used in summer bedding schemes.

Because dahlias are named after Andreas Dahl (a pupil of Linnaeus), the correct pronunciation should be "doll-ia".

Bloomtime: May to frost.

Height: 12–15 inches (30–38 cm) for bedding cultivars.

Light and soil: Dahlias require full sun and rich, well-drained, fertile soil that does not dry out. Do not use a high-nitrogen fertilizer.

How to grow: Bedding plants are available in garden shops in spring. To grow them from seed, sow in early March and cover seeds lightly with soil. At 60–70°F (15–21°C), germination takes 10 days. Grow on at 55°F (13°C). Set plants out 12 inches (30 cm) apart in May. Remove dead flowers to encourage bloom and to tidy plants. (Take care when deadheading, as the old and new flower buds look alike. The old buds are more pointed and softer when gently squeezed). Bedding dahlias form tuberous roots during the growing season and may be overwintered. Cut stems to 4 inches (10 cm) and dig roots. Allow them to dry, then store them in boxes covered with peat in a cool, dry, frost-free place. In March, bring them out into the light and allow growth to begin. Divide if desired, ensuring that each section has one shoot and a piece of the original stem. Plant out in April. Dahlias can survive a mild winter if left in the ground, but they should be dug and divided in spring.

Pests and diseases: APHIDS sometimes infest new growth, and EARWIGS hide in the flowers and eat holes in the leaves and petals.

Uses: Beds and borders; mixed planter boxes; long-lasting cut flowers.

"Daisy, African" see *Dimorphotheca, Gazania* and *Osteospermum*
"Daisy, blue" see *Felicia*
"Daisy, gloriosa" see *Rudbeckia*
"Daisy, Livingstone" see *Cleretum*
"Daisy, marguerite" see *Chrysanthemum frutescens*
"Daisy, Swan River" see *Brachycome*
"Daisy, Transvaal" see *Gerbera*

Dianthus barbatus "sweet william"
Dianthus chinensis "China pink"
Dianthus caryophyllus "carnation" CARYOPHYLLACEAE
(Figures 3-3, 4-4 and 4-5)

I have always found this genus to be a bit confusing, so I felt heartened to read the following quotation of an ancient scholar in the delightful book *Flowers, A Guide for Your Garden,* by Pizzetti and Cocker: "If I had the memory of Themistocles, who greeted every citizen by name; of Cyrus and of Scipio, who knew the names of all their soldiers; if I could, like Cineas, ambassador of Pyrrhus, name every senator and every citizen of Rome; it

1-1 *Abutilon hybridum*
flowering maple

1-2 *Amaranthus tricolor*
Joseph's coat

1-3 *Antirrhinum majus*
'Kolibri Mixed'
dwarf snapdragon

1-4 *Begonia xtuberhybrida*
'Nonstop'
upright tuberous begonias

1-5 *Canna xgeneralis*
'The President'
canna lily

1-6 *Celosia cristata*
'Apricot Brandy'
cockscomb

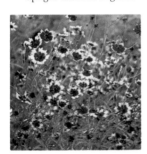

1-7 *Coreopsis tinctoria*
'Single Dwarf Mixed'
calliopsis

1-8 *Cuphea ignea*
cigar flower

1-9 *Mimulus* hybrids
'Calypso Mixed'
monkey flower

1-10 *Nemesia strumosa*
'Carnival Blend'
nemesia

1-11 *Tropaeolum majus*
'Glorious Gleam Mixture'
nasturtium

2-1 *Begonia xsemp.-cultorum*
'Prelude Pink'
fibrous begonia

2-2 *Brachycome iberidifolia*
Swan River daisy

2-3 *Cleome hasslerana*
'Rose Queen'
spider flower

2-4 *Coleus xhybridus*
'Carefree Mixed'
coleus

2-5 *Felicia amelloides*
blue marguerite

2-6 *Impatiens wallerana*
'Super Elfin Blush'
common impatiens

2-7 *Limonium sinuatum*
'Pacific Mixed'
statice

2-8 *Lychnis coeli-rosa*
viscaria

2-9 *Nemophila menziesii*
baby blue eyes

2-10 *Nigella damascena*
love-in-a-mist

2-11 *Torenia fournieri*
'Compacta'
wishbone flower

3-1 *Callistephus chinensis*
'Pinocchio Mix'
China aster

3-2 *Cleretum bellidiformis*
Livingstone daisy

3-3 *Dianthus chinensis*
'Telstar'
China pink

3-4 *Helichrysum bracteatum*
'Semidwarf Mixed'
strawflower

3-5 *Lathyrus odoratus*
'Bolton's Old Fashioned'
sweet pea

3-6 *Lavatera trimestris*
'Silver Cup'
mallow

3-7 *Matthiola incana*
'East Lothian Mixed'
stock

3-8 *Pelargonium peltatum*
ivy geraniums

3-9 *Phlox drummondii*
'Dwarf Beauty Mix'
annual phlox

3-10 *Viola xwittrockiana*
'Universal Red'
pansy

3-11 *Xeranthemum annuum*
common immortelle

4-1 *Clarkia amoena*
'Dwarf Azalea Flowered'
godetia

4-2 *Cosmos bipinnatus*
'Sensation Mixed'
cosmos

4-3 *Dahlia* 'Rigoletto'
dahlia

4-4 *Dianthus barbatus*
sweet william

4-5 *Dianthus caryophyllus*
'Grenadin Mixed'
carnation

4-6 *Fuchsia xhybrida*
'Empress of Prussia'
fuchsia

4-7 *Portulaca grandiflora*
'Calypso Mixed'
moss rose

4-8 *Salvia splendens*
'St. John's Fire'
red salvia

4-9 *Schizanthus* hybrids
'Hit Parade Mixed'
butterfly flower

4-10 *Verbena canadensis*
trailing verbena

4-11 *Zinnia elegans*
'Peter Pan Mixed'
zinnia

5-1 *Ageratum houstonianum*
'Blue Blazer'
flossflower

5-2 *Brassica oleracea*
'Snow Prince' (l)
and purple kale (r),

5-3 *Browallia speciosa*
'Marine Bells'
browallia

5-4 *Catananche caerulea*
cupid's dart

5-5 *Centaurea cyanus*
bachelor's button

5-6 *Gomphrena globosa*
'Mixed'
globe amaranth

Morgan Jones

5-7 *Impatiens* 'Gemini'
New Guinea impatiens

5-8 *Nierembergia hipp.*
var. *violacea*
'Purple Robe' cupflower

5-9 *Petunia xhybrida*
'Falcon Blue'
multiflora petunia

5-10 *Salpiglossis sinuata*
'Bolero Mixed'
salpiglossis

5-11 *Salvia farinacea*
'Victoria'
blue salvia

6-1 *Amaranthus caudatus*
love-lies-bleeding

6-2 *Chrysanthemum frutescens*
marguerite daisy

6-3 *Cordyline australis*
dracaena palm
in center of barrel

6-4 *Glechoma hederacea*
'Variegata'
nepeta

6-5 *Hedera helix*
'Glacier'
English ivy

6-6 *Hypoestes phyllostachya*
'Pink Splash'
polka dot plant

6-7 *Kochia scoparia*
forma *trichophylla*
summer cypress

6-8 *Lobelia erinus*
trailing lobeia on left

6-9 *Lotus berthelotii*
lotus vine

6-10 *Senecio cineraria*
'Diamond' dusty miller
with 'Matador' geraniums

6-11 *Thunbergia alata*
black-eyed-susan vine

7-1 *Calceolaria* 'Goldri'
    pocketbook flower

7-2 *Chrysanthemum parthenium*
    'Gold Ball'
    feverfew or matricaria

7-3 *Dimorphotheca* hybrids
    African daisy or
    star-of-the-veldt

7-4 *Erysimum hieraciifolium*
    Siberian wallflower

7-5 *Gazania xhybrida*
    'Chansonette'
    gazania

7-6 *Helianthus annuus*
    'Teddy Bear'
    sunflower

7-7 *Lantana camara* with
    blue salvia, marguerites
    and geraniums

7-8 *Papaver nudicaule*
    'Champagne Bubbles'
    Iceland poppy

7-9 *Primula xpolyantha*
    polyanthus

7-10 *Rudbeckia hirta*
     'Marmalade'
     black-eyed susan

7-11 *Tagetes erecta*
     'Gold Lady'
     African marigold

7-12 *Tagetes patula*
     'Nell Gwyn'
     French marigold

8-1 *Calendula officinalis*
'Fiesta Gitana'
English marigold

8-2 *Chrysanthemum carinatum*
annual chrysanthemum

8-3 *Heliotropium arborescens*
fragrant heliotrope with geraniums

8-4 *Lobularia maritima*
'New Carpet of Snow'
sweet alyssum

8-5 *Molucella laevis*
bells of Ireland

8-6 Moss basket with
'Lemon Gem' marigolds,
lobelia & geraniums

8-7 *Nicotiana alata*
'Domino Mix'
flowering tobacco

8-8 *Osteospermum ecklonis*
African daisy

8-9 *Pelargonium xdomesticum*
'Aztec'
regal pelargonium

8-10 *Pelargonium xhortorum*
'Petals'
fancy leaf geranium

8-11 *Verbena xhybrida*
'Sandy White'
garden verbena

would still be impossible for me, entering a garden, to know all the dianthus by name."

There is confusion regarding the exact number of species in the genus *Dianthus* due to the variability of species and the ease with which they hybridize. Botanists generally set the number at 300. In the area of bedding plants there are mainly three types on the market.

Sweet williams have a variable life-cycle, being annuals, biennials or short-lived perennials from southern Europe. They can be started from seed in the summer and planted out into their flowering positions in the fall, where they will bloom in spring. Seeds may be started indoors in March, for bloom the same year. 'Double Flowered Mixed' grows to 18 inches (46 cm) and has about 60 percent double blooms. 'Indian Carpet' is a mix of single flowers in scarlet, crimson, pink, or white, often with a contrasting eye; they grow to 6 inches (15 cm). 'Wee Willie' blooms the first year from seed in June and July and is a very dwarf 4 inches (10 cm). It is usually available in shops in spring with the bedding plants. 'Double Flowered Mixed' and 'Indian Carpet' are often sold with the perennials.

Cultivars of *Dianthus chinensis*, **China pinks**, also bloom the first year from seed. 'Snowfire' makes a very eye-catching display in early summer with showy white 1½- to 2-inch (4- to 5-cm) blooms with red centers. Plants grow to 8 inches (20 cm) high. 'Telstar' (a Fleuroselect winner with scarlet blooms) and 'Princess Mixed' bloom all summer. They are half-hardy.

Young **carnation** plants, *Dianthus caryophyllus,* are available in spring with the bedding plants or with perennials. Bedding cultivars (often referred to as annual carnations) bloom from July on from a February sowing, are excellent cut flowers and have attractive silver foliage. 'Giant Chabaud Mixed' grows to 24 inches (61 cm) high; staking is required. 'Knight Series Mixed' has very strong stems and a wide range of colors. The most outstanding annual carnation in the bedding plant trials is 'Scarlet Luminette' (a Fleuroselect winner), which is deeply fragrant and makes a wonderful cut flower. Carnations are native to Europe.

Bloomtime: Refer to each type above.

Height: 4–24 inches (10–61 cm), depending on the cultivar.

Light and soil: Full sun and well-drained soil to which some organic matter has been added. All dianthus like a sweet soil; add lime if the pH is below 6.5, which it usually is in our rainy coastal region.

How to grow: Young plants of many cultivars are generally available from shops in spring, or they may be started from seed. See notes above for each type, but generally they should be sown in February or March. Germination, at 70°F (21°C) soil temperature, takes about 21 days.

Planting distance: Sweet williams: 8–10 inches (20–25 cm); Indian pinks: 6–9 inches (15–23 cm); bedding carnations: 12 inches (30 cm).

Pests and diseases: APHIDS and CATERPILLARS may attack the leaves and new shoots.

Uses: Dwarf sweet william might be used at the front of a border, in a rock garden or in containers. Taller sweet william is suitable for a mixed border or larger container. (In a container on its own, it might be moved to a resting place when not in bloom.) Plant China pinks in mixed borders and in containers. Carnations look attractive in a mixed border, or, if you plan to cut them heavily, use a cutting garden or part of the vegetable garden.

***Dimorphotheca* hybrids** "African daisy" "star-of-the-veldt" "Cape marigold" "dimorphotheca" ASTERACEAE
(Figure 7-3)

African daisies form a mat of 12-inch (30-cm) stems topped by blooms in shades of orange, yellow and cream, each with a dark disk at the center. The leaves, to 3½ inches (9 cm) long, have several small teeth along the edge. The dimorphothecas listed in seed catalogues and sold in shops are hybrids of two annuals from South Africa, *D. pluvialis* and *D. sinuata* (*D. aurantiaca*). Both love full sun and hot, dry locations, making them excellent additions to a rock garden. Some gardeners report dimorphothecas surviving a mild winter unprotected, but because they are annual, it is more likely that they have reseeded themselves.

The seed mixture 'Tetra Goliath' is an early bloomer with dense plants and 3½-inch (9-cm) blooms. 'Starshine' has 2- to 3-inch (5- to 8-cm) blooms in shades of carmine, pink, rose and white on plants which can spread up to 18 inches (46 cm) across. If you have the space to start them from seed, these would be worth a try, as the more commonly available 'Aurantiaca Mixed' have small flowers that are not as showy.

The name comes from the Greek and means "two shapes of seeds" (*dimorpho-theca*). This refers to the curious nature of this plant: the outer ray florets (see page 51) develop into seeds that look like minute sticks, while the central disk florets develop into larger flattened seeds.

Plants of another African daisy, osteospermum, are often sold as dimorphotheca. See that entry also for further information.

Bloomtime: June to frost, flowers opening on sunny days only. They don't hold up well in the rain, so in a very wet summer they may not look their best.

Height: 12–16 inches (30–41 cm).
Light and soil: Full sun with well-drained, sandy soil. They tolerate dry soil.
How to grow: Sometimes available in shops in May, they are also easily grown from seed. Sow outdoors in mid-April, spacing seeds 8 inches (20 cm) apart (or sow indoors in March). Cover the seeds with a very thin layer of sand. Although some books say seedlings are not easy to transplant, I know of several gardeners who have had no problems with transplanting. Set out plants in late May.
Planting distance: 8 inches (20 cm).
Pests and diseases: Leaves may be affected by GRAY MOLD in very wet weather.
Uses: Front of border, rock garden, dry places in the garden.

"Dracaena palm" see *Cordyline*
"Dusty miller" see *Senecio*
Erysimum hieraciifolium see *Cheiranthus*

Felicia amelloides "blue marguerite" "blue daisy" "felicia" ASTERACEAE
(Figure 2-5)
In its native South Africa, the blue marguerite is a subshrub, but in the Pacific coast area it doesn't survive most winters. The plant is well-branched with attractive, rounded, 1-inch (2½-cm) leaves that are slightly rough to the touch. The small blue flowers are 1 inch (2½ cm) across with a yellow center. Because the flowers are small, they are not showy, but they have a delicate beauty that adds much to the garden.
Bloomtime: June until the frost, flowers open on sunny days.
Height: 12–24 inches (30–61 cm).
Light and soil: Full sun and well-drained soil to which some organic matter has been added.
How to grow: Generally available from shops in May, blue marguerites can also be grown from seed started indoors in March or April at 60°F (15°C). Pinch out the growing tips when the plants are about four inches (10 cm) high to encourage branching and more flowers. Plant out at the end of May, 9 inches (23 cm) apart. New plants can also be started from cuttings made from June to September. Plants can be dug and overwintered in a greenhouse or sunroom.
Pests and diseases: Generally trouble-free.

Uses: At the front of beds and mixed borders; in sunny spots in rock gardens; in planters and hanging baskets, alone or with other bedding plants.

"Feverfew" see *Chrysanthemum parthenium*
"Firecracker plant" see *Cuphea*
"Flossflower" see *Ageratum*
"Flowering tobacco" see *Nicotiana*
"Forget-me-not" see *Myosotis*
"Four-o'clock" see *Mirabilis*

Fuchsia x*hybrida* "fuchsia" ONAGRACEAE
(Figures 4-6 and 6-8)

Fuchsias are so popular that, like geraniums and begonias, there are special clubs devoted to their cultivation. The flowers, which hang from the tips of the stems, have a long tube that opens out into four sepals. These enclose the bud like a balloon until it opens, then extend sideways or curve backwards above the flower. There are four petals in single species and cultivars, but more in double cultivars; these petals are sometimes referred to as the corolla or "skirt." The stamens and style extend below the petals, adding a delicate touch. The color range includes combinations of white, pink, red, rose, violet and purple. Cultivars have been developed from many species, the main three being *Fuchsia fulgens, F. magellanica* and *F. triphylla*.

Fuchsias are half-hardy shrubs from the mountain woodlands of Central and South America, and they enjoy the cool nights of Pacific coast summers. Most fuchsias need protection from the frost and must be overwintered in a greenhouse or sunroom. Some cultivars, indicated on the following table, are hardy enough to survive most winters. (The tops die down, but the roots send up new shoots in spring.) These cultivars also seem to be more sun-tolerant. I have seen 'Double Otto', 'Empress of Prussia' and 'Riccartonii' thriving in full sun all day. Hardy fuchsias grow up to 3 feet (1 m) tall.

Some fuchsias grow upright, while others have a trailing habit. The trailing cultivars are perfect for growing in hanging baskets, where their flowers may be more fully appreciated. Cultivars marked both upright and trailing have a wide-growing habit and are suitable for bushy plants or for container planting. They will not trail straight down, but will grow over the edges. Following are some popular fuchsia cultivars.

Name	sepals	petals	single	double	trailing	upright	hardy	standards
Bicentennial	orange	dark orange		•	•			•
Dark Eyes	red	dark blue		•	•			•
Display	rosy-red	cerise	•			•		
Dollar Princess	cerise	purple		•		•	•	
Double Otto	red	purple		•		•	•	
Empress of Prussia	scarlet	magenta	•			•	•	
Gartenmeister Bonstedt*	orange-red	orange-red	•			•		
Indian Maid	red recurving	purple		•	•			•
Jack Shahan	pink	pink	•		•	•		•
Lena	pale pink	magenta		•	•	•		•
Lisa	blue	pink		•	•			•**
Marinka	red	red	•		•			•
Miss California	pink recurving	pale pink	•			•		•
Mrs. Popple	red	navy blue	•			•	•	•
Papoose	red	dark purple	•			•	•	
Peppermint Stick	carmine recurving	violet		•		•		
Pink Galore	pink	pink		•	•			
Pink Marshmallow	white recurving	white flushed pink			•			•
Riccartoni	scarlet	violet	•			•	•	
Snowcap	red	white		•		•		•
Swingtime	red	white		•	•			•
Winston Churchill	red recurving	magenta wavy		•		•		

Cultivars marked under standard are suitable for training as standards.
* dark olive green foliage takes full sun
** very slow-growing, thus taking longer to make a standard than some cultivars

Training standard fuchsias. Fuchsia trees–standard fuchsias–are fuchsias that have been trained to form a trunk by staking and pruning. An elegant addition to a bed or planter, they are available in shops in spring. You can train a fuchsia quite easily provided you have a place to overwinter it, as it takes a full year. Start with a soft plastic pot (the kind used in nurseries) 8 inches wide by 12 inches deep (20 cm by 30 cm). Secure a 4-foot (1.2-m) cedar stake to the pot by nailing the stake to a cross-piece and nailing the cross-piece to the pot. To make a fuller crown on the tree, two fuchsia plants of the same cultivar are used. (Branches and roots of the two plants will intermingle.)

Use a potting mix that is rich in organic matter, but has some sand to add weight, otherwise plants will easily tip over when full-grown. Plant one fuchsia on either side of the cedar stake. As the plants grow, gently secure the tip of each fuchsia to its own side of the stake with a piece of soft green plastic sold for tying plants. The object of this training is to get two straight stems, with the stake between them for support. This will form the trunk for the fuchsia tree. As the plants grow, they will send out side shoots, which should be shortened to two leaf nodes. Do not remove the large leaves that grow along the main stems.

When the plants have grown to within 2 inches (5 cm) of the top of the stake, pinch out the growing tips to encourage branching. Do not let the main stems grow taller than the stake, because then they can no longer be tied to it for support. When the crown develops and becomes heavy with bloom, the whole crown could snap off. As the crown develops, keep pinching the growing tips to encourage branching. It takes about six months to train the trunks up the stake and another six months for a well-branched crown to develop.

Cultivars suitable for training as standards are indicated in the table above. 'Miss California' is particularly attractive as a standard, but 'Lena' requires a lot of fussing and 'Lisa' is slow growing.

Bloomtime: May to frost, looking great in the fall if well cared for.

Height: 12–24 inches (30–61 cm), upright or trailing, depending on the cultivar.

Light and soil: Although some cultivars will take sun, most prefer filtered or afternoon shade. Plant in a well-drained soil to which some moist peat has been added.

How to grow: Plants are readily available in shops in spring. For fancy cultivars, contact your local fuchsia society; they usually have annual sales. Set plants out at the end of May or early June. Keep them moist or the flower buds may drop. Remove old flowers and fertilize weekly with a liquid fertilizer. Early in the season, a balanced fertilizer such as 20-20-20 may be used to encourage growth, but by July use a formulation with more phosphorous to encourage bloom.

Fuchsia plants which are several years old produce an abundance of bloom, so overwinter plants if possible. To do this, gradually withhold water from plants in mid-October to force them into dormancy. All the leaves will fall, and the plants should not be watered again until spring. Store them in a cool, 55°F (13°C), but not necessarily bright, place. Check the plants from time to time; if the stems start to wither, spray them with tepid water. In March, soak the pots in water. This will cause the buds to swell and you may then prune the plants. Cut each stem back to just above the sixth node, approximately. After pruning, remove the plants from the pot, shaking off all old soil. Rinse roots and repot with fresh potting mix. Water well and place them in a bright window or greenhouse. On warm days, put the plants outside, out of direct sunlight, to harden off. Set them out in late May. After three years, the plants should be thrown away.

Fuchsias can also be grown from from seed, or from cuttings taken in August or September and kept over winter. Seedlings won't be true to the parent, but it can be fun. To grow fuchsias from seed, allow some flowers to develop berries. (Not all cultivars will set berries.) Break up very ripe, soft berries into a bowl of water and clean the seeds, dry them on paper towels and store in a cool, dry place. Plant in spring or fall in soil 55°F (13°C) or warmer. The germination rate is normally very good.

For suggestions on using fuchsias in hanging baskets, see Chapter 6.

Pests and diseases: APHIDS sometimes suck the sap of leaves and stems. SLUGS eat the new shoots of hardy fuchsias. SPIDER MITES can infest the underside of the leaves. WHITEFLY may be a problem in the greenhouse. A PHYSIOLOGICAL DISORDER causes yellow and purple spots and the leaves later fall off.

Uses: Fuchsia is a classic for hanging baskets, either alone or mixed with other bedding plants. Use in planters and use upright cultivars in borders.

Gazania x*hybrida* "gazania" "African daisy" ASTERACEAE
(Figures 6-3 and 7-5)

Gazanias are another daisy-like flower from South African and, like the two other African daisies, they like a warm spot in full sun, and the flowers open only on sunny days. Gazanias come in shades of yellow, mahogany, tangerine, red, white, pink and orange, and often have rings of contrasting color. The leaves form a rosette around the base of the short stems. Although gazanias are perennial in warmer climates, they do not survive the winter in the Pacific coast region.

The 'Mini-Star' series is available in separate colors, the 'Tangerine Mini-Star' won AAS and Fleuroselect awards; 'Mini-star Yellow' was a Fleuroselect winner. 'Sundance' has flowers of mixed colors, including one that has red and yellow striped petals; it grows quickly from seed. 'Carnival', has stunningly marked and colored flowers and silvery foliage.

Bloomtime: May to frost.

Height: 6–8 inches (15–20 cm).

Light and soil: Full sun and a well-drained soil to which some organic matter has been added. Gazanias tolerate dry soil.

How to grow: Young plants are generally available from shops in spring, or they may be started from seed. Sow in February. Germination is erratic, and it is essential to use only fresh seeds. Set young plants out in late May, 12 inches (30 cm) apart. Remove faded flowers. Plants may be started from cuttings taken in August or September and inserted into very sandy soil. Plants may also be increased by division.

Pests and diseases: In very wet weather, GRAY MOLD may be a problem.

Uses: Its low-growing, almost trailing habit makes gazania a perfect candidate for rock gardens, pockets in a rock wall or the edge of an informal mixed border. Use in containers or hanging baskets, alone or with other bedding plants.

"Geranium, ivy or trailing" see *Pelargonium peltatum*
"Geranium, Martha Washington or pansy" see *Pelargonium xdomesticum*
"Geranium, zonal" see *Pelargonium xhortorum*

Gerbera jamesonii "gerbera daisy" "Transvaal daisy" ASTERACEAE

Gerbera daisies are often sold in stores in spring and are very tempting, but they are a tricky plant to grow–particularly to water correctly–and for that reason are not recommended as good bedding plants in this area. They are best suited to a cool greenhouse or container under cover, where their watering and care can be more easily controlled.

Glechoma hederacea '**Variegata**' (*Nepeta hederacea*) "nepeta" LAMIACEAE
(Figures 6-4 and 8-6)

Nepeta is a creeping evergreen perennial native to Europe and Asia. It is a "must" for hanging baskets, with its long, trailing stems covered with round, green and white leaves. The fine stems are very effective as they move in the breeze. Nepeta also works well trailing from window boxes and planters.

Bloomtime: Although grown for its foliage, it has small, lilac, pea-like flowers.

Height: Trailing stems as long as 4 feet (1.2 m) by the end of summer.

Light and soil: Full sun or light shade and any well-drained soil.

How to grow: Young plants are generally available from shops in spring, or they may be started from cuttings taken at almost any time. Large clumps may also be divided in fall or spring. Nepeta will survive a mild winter; plants may be taken into a garage for extra protection during very cold

spells, but don't let them dry out.
Pests and diseases: MILDEW is occasionally a problem.
Uses: Hanging baskets; containers; trailing over retaining walls.

"Globe amaranth" see *Gomphrena*
"Godetia" see *Clarkia*

Gomphrena globosa "globe amaranth"
Gomphrena haageana AMARANTHACEAE
(Figure 5-6)

Gomphrena globosa is a half-hardy annual native to India. In Thailand, its flowers are used in dried arrangements for weddings. Wreaths are made with a circle of wet clay into which the flower heads are stuck. When the clay dries, the flowers retain their rich color indefinitely. The cultivar 'Buddy' has flowers of a vivid royal purple, one of those colors people seem to either love or hate. It grows to a uniform height of 9 inches (23 cm) and makes a good edging plant. There are also seed strains of mixed colors, but the white is not a pure white and is not as striking as the purple.

Gomphrena haageana is a perennial native to Texas and Mexico. Its cultivar 'Strawberry Fields' is grown as an annual on the Pacific coast. Flowers are bright red and the plant grows to 2 feet (.6 m).
Bloomtime: July to September.
Height: 9–24 inches (23–61 cm), depending on the cultivar.
Light and soil: Full sun and well-drained soil that is not too rich.
How to grow: Although young plants are not generally available from shops, they are easily grown from seed. In April, soak the seeds in water for 3 days and then spread them thinly over the top of the soil. Germinate at 70°F (21°C) for 14 days in total darkness. Grow on at 70°F (21°C). Set hardened-off plants out in late May or early June, 6–9 inches (15–23 cm) apart, farther for 'Strawberry Fields'.
Pests and diseases: APHIDS may infest new shoots.
Uses: Use 'Buddy' to edge beds and borders, 'Strawberry Fields' in mixed borders and for flower arrangements, fresh or dried. All flowers dry very well with no special treatment; the flowers of 'Buddy' do not have long stems but can be used to decorate wreaths. Children enjoy them in various crafts.

"Grasses" see *Avena*
"Hare's tail" see *Avena*

Hedera helix "English ivy" ARALIACEAE
(Figure 6-5)

An all-purpose plant for the garden, ivy is included here because it is an excellent addition to a hanging basket or planter. There are several cultivars with small leaves that are often sold with the bedding plants in shops in spring. You may also find them with the ground covers or with the houseplants. English ivy, a native of Britain and Europe, is evergreen and survives the winter outdoors. Three of the many culitvars are 'Baltica', with dark green leaves and distinctive white veins; 'Glacier', with gray-green leaves and a white margin, and 'Gold Heart', which has a yellow heart-shaped blotch in the middle of each leaf.

Bloomtime: Grown for its foliage, ivy doesn't flower until it is many years of age. The flowers look like green pompons 1 inch (2.5 cm) across.

Height: Growing as a creeper or vine, ivy grows 1–2 feet (30–61 cm) each year.

Light and soil: Full sun to heavy shade. Ivy will grow in any soil, but grows faster in a rich soil.

How to grow: Young plants are generally available from shops in spring, or they may be started from cuttings taken at any time of the year. It is possible to take them in March and stick them right in the soil in the garden, where they will root if the weather is wet.

Pests and diseases: Generally trouble-free.

Uses: Trailing out of planters and hanging baskets, with summer or winter bedding.

Helianthus annuus "sunflower" ASTERACEAE
(Figure 7-6)

Helianthus translates from the Greek into "sunflower," a name given to these huge plants because the flowers of some cultivars turn toward the sun. Once seeds begin to form, the flowers stop moving, usually all facing in an easterly direction. Commercial sunflower growers take advantage of this, planting sunflowers in north/south rows—it makes harvesting easier when almost all the heads are facing into the row.

It is thought that the first *Helianthus* seeds were imported from Mexico and grown in the Madrid Royal Gardens in 1562. Many parts of the plants have economic importance: the seeds are delicious, both to people and birds, and cooking oil is produced from the seed. The leaves may be used as animal forage and the Chinese make a textile from the plant fibers. In the garden, sunflowers are a tremendous hit with children because they grow to 8 feet (2½ m) or more in height, their huge blooms facing downward.

The leaves are heart shaped, up to 15 inches (38 cm) long and hairy on both surfaces. Sunflowers are hardy annuals native to the United States, Canada and Mexico. In 1910, a Mrs. Cockerell found a chestnut-colored sunflower growing on the roadside in Boulder, Colorado. From this, she developed many variously colored cultivars.

'Italian White' has cream petals with a black center; it reaches 4 feet (1.2 m) and blooms are 4 inches (10 cm) across. 'Large Flowered Mixed' has 6-inch (15-cm) blooms of many colors on 5-foot (1.5-m) plants. 'Teddy Bear' grows to only 2 feet (61 cm) and has double blooms. There are also a number of giant cultivars.

Bloomtime: July to October.

Height: 2–10 feet (.6–3 m), depending on the cultivar.

Light and soil: Prefers full sun and any well-drained soil. It has surprisingly small roots for such a tall plant, so staking is a good idea, especially in windy places.

How to grow: Although young plants are not generally available from shops, they are easily grown from seed. Sow seeds directly in the garden in April, or indoors in March. Plants should be spaced 12–18 inches (30–46 cm) apart.

Pests and diseases: Generally trouble-free.

Uses: Sunflowers are popular with children and fun for gardeners of all ages. 'Teddy Bear' makes an interesting centerpiece to a large planter.

Helichrysum bracteatum "strawflower" ASTERACEAE

(Figure 3-4)

Native to Australia, strawflowers "have the dubious distinction of being equally attractive dead or alive," write Pizzetti and Cocker. This is certainly true: the plants themselves are an attractive addition to a mixed border in the garden and they are everlasting when dried. The leaves are long, narrow and bright green. Blooms come in soft shades of pink, gold, yellow or cream, as well as more brightly colored cultivars. Seed is available as separate colors or in mixtures. 'Hot Bikinis' won a Fleuroselect award. Watch for a new cultivar of dwarf strawflower that can be used as an edging and still be dried.

Bloomtime: June to frost.

Height: 3–4 feet (.9–1.2 m).

Light and soil: Prefers full sun and any well-drained soil that is neutral or slightly sweet.

How to grow: Although young plants are not generally available from shops, they are easily grown from seed. Sow seeds indoors in March, but do not cover, as light is required for germination. Germination, at 70°F (21°C) soil temperature, takes 10–14 days. Grow plants on at 70°F (21°C). Set hardened-off plants out in late May, spacing them 12 inches (30 cm) apart. Alternatively, seeds may be sown directly in the garden in May. Pick the flowers before the colored bracts open to reveal the disk. If picked when the bracts are fully open, the disk florets will form seeds and the flower will fall apart. The stems become quite dry and brittle, so it is worthwhile removing the stems after picking and inserting thin florist's wire from the back up through the flowers before letting them dry. Using pliers, bend the end of the wire over and gently pull it back into the flower. The flowers may then be used on the wires instead of stems.

Pests and diseases: Generally trouble-free.

Uses: Attractive in a mixed border or in a large planter. If you plan to cut them constantly, you may wish to plant strawflowers in the cutting or vegetable garden. Popular with children, they are lovely for decorating wreaths and other craft projects.

Heliotropium arborescens "heliotrope" "cherry pie" BORAGINACEAE (Figure 8-3)

Heliotrope was first discovered in Peru, where it is a perennial, in 1740. It was sent to Paris, where it was popular for flower arrangements and was dubbed the herbe d'amour (plant of love). Commonly grown by the British during Queen Victoria's time, it was popular for its rich fragrance. The Victorians called it "cherry pie" because it smells as sweet as a freshly baked cherry pie. The fragrance is also reminiscent of vanilla. Heliotrope was once planted in fields of tomatoes and cucumbers to attract bees for pollination. It has an open, spreading habit and mid-green leaves. The light violet flowers are arranged on a curved spike.

Strangely enough, heliotrope went out of style and virtually disappeared from the bedding plant market. Although grown in Butchart Gardens on Vancouver Island and in Stanley Park in Vancouver, BC, from cuttings for over forty years, the only cultivars available to home gardeners were those which could be grown from seed. 'Marine', for example, develops into good-looking plants with deep purple broccoli-like flower heads and deep purplish-green leaves, but the blooms are generally not fragrant. With the current interest in fragrant plants, the type of heliotrope grown from cuttings should become more available.

Bloomtime: June to October.

Height: 12–24 inches (30–61 cm), depending on the cultivar.

Light and soil: Full sun or light shade. They need a very rich soil to flourish, so add lots of organic matter and some general fertilizer.

How to grow: Although young plants are not generally available from shops, some types may be grown from seed (see above). There are several seed strains on the market which claim to be fragrant. Sow seeds in February at 70°F (21°C).Germination is not always good and may take up to three weeks. Pinch back young plants to encourage branching. Set plants out 12 inches (30 cm) apart into the garden or into containers in late May or early June. Fertilize regularly. If you get a seedling which is particularly fragrant, keep it through the winter indoors. Although hard to find, try a specialty nursery for cuttings of the fragrant heliotrope.

Pests and diseases: Generally trouble-free in the garden. In the greenhouse, plants may get WHITEFLY.

Uses: Cultivars such as 'Marine' look good in mixed planters with other bedding plants. Try it with dwarf marigolds and ageratum, or with white browallia and orange gazanias. The very fragrant type is good in hanging baskets and in beds with plants such as geraniums and French marigolds. Heliotrope may also be trained as a standard. See instructions under *Fuchsia*.

Hypoestes phyllostachya (*H. sanguinolenta*) "polka dot plant"
ACANTHACEAE
(Figure 6-6)

A perennial from Madagascar, the polka dot plant is usually grown and sold as a houseplant, but it is possible to grow it as a bedding plant. In the garden it makes a bushy plant, its rich olive green leaves spotted and splashed with pink. At the end of September, it looks as fresh as in June. In my experience, it received virtually no attention except for watering and had no diseases or pests. 'Pink Splash' has the largest pink spots of available cultivars.

Bloomtime: Although grown for its decorative foliage, polka dot plant develops tiny purple tubular flowers in late summer.

Height: To 16 inches (41 cm).

Light and soil: Full sun, partial shade or shade, in well-drained soil.

How to grow: Young plants are generally available from shops with houseplants. It is also easy to grow from seed sown indoors in early April. Set out hardened-off plants in late May or June, depending on the season. Plants may be dug up and brought back indoors before the frost and grown in a sunny window.

Pests and diseases: Generally trouble-free.

Uses: Edging plant for beds and borders. Pots and planter boxes, alone or with other bedding plants. Hypoestes and pink tuberous or fibrous begonias make a striking combination.

Iberis amara "hyacinth-flowered candytuft" "rocket candytuft"
Iberis umbellata "globe candytuft" BRASSICACEAE

These two candytufts bloom from May to July and, if allowed to seed themselves, reappear each year. Both are hardy annuals from Europe and rocket candytuft has been grown as a garden plant since the sixteenth century. It is a striking plant; the tiny white flowers form along a tall spike that resembles a hyacinth. It is also fragrant. Globe candytuft bears its tiny flowers in flat-topped clusters over a neat mound-shaped plant. Most seed mixtures include white, maroon, lilac and rose flowers. Globe candytuft has no fragrance. The leaves are narrow and midgreen.

Bloomtime: May to July, unless later sowings are made to extend the season of bloom.

Height: Rocket candytuft, 12–24 inches (30–61 cm); globe candytuft 12–15 inches (30–38 cm).

Light and soil: Full sun and any well-drained soil. They will tolerate dry soil, but not "wet feet."

How to grow: The best way to grow these is to seed them in October where they are to flower. Throw more seeds out in March, April and June to have blooms until fall. They may also be started indoors from March on and set out from May on. Thin seedlings or space young plants 6 to 9 inches (15–23 cm) apart.

Pests and diseases: Generally trouble-free.

Uses: Use rocket candytuft in mixed flower borders and for cutting. Globe candytuft is good for edging and at the front of mixed borders. Use with plants such as browallia and geraniums, which will fill in the gap they leave later in the summer.

"Ice plant" see *Lampranthus*
"Immortelle, common" see *Xeranthemum*

***Impatiens* hybrids** "New Guinea impatiens" BALSAMINACEAE
(Figure 5-7)

Quite different in many ways from common impatiens (see below), these exotic plants not only have beautiful flowers, but also decorative leaves. They like full sun or part shade, but do not bloom well in full shade. The flowers are up to 3 inches (7.5 cm) across and the leaves are long and pointed at the tip. They are dark green, often with a yellow center to the leaf and a dark red midrib.

New Guinea impatiens are a relatively recent arrival on the bedding plant market. In the winter of 1969–70, a team of American plant collectors went to New Guinea, looking for orchids, rhododendrons and pitcher plants. The trip was sponsored jointly by the US Department of Agriculture and Longwood Gardens in Pennsylvania. In the damp cool forests of New Guinea, about 3,300 feet (1,000 m) above sea level, they found 25 interesting types of impatiens. They sent cuttings back to Dr. Robert Armstrong, a horticultural researcher at Longwood Gardens, who made crosses between several of the species. This first generation of crosses, known as F_1 hybrids, were outstanding and inspired the breeding program which has produced the dozens of New Guinea impatiens now available.

Most New Guinea impatiens are grown from cuttings. 'Gemini' is an excellent cultivar with pink flowers and green and yellow foliage. New Guinea impatiens may also be grown from seed (for example the seed mixture 'Sweet Sue'), but plants tend to be leggier than those grown from cuttings.

Bloomtime: June to frost.

Height: To 18 inches (46 cm).

Light and soil: Full sun to light shade; in full shade they will grow but will be leggier and have fewer blooms. New Guinea impatiens prefer a light soil to which moist peat or well-rotted manure has been added. Keep them well fertilized and watered.

How to grow: The easiest way to grow New Guinea impatiens is to buy young plants, generally available from shops in spring. They may also be started from 3–4 inch (7.5–10 cm) tip cuttings taken April to September and rooted in peat and perlite at 60°F (15°C) soil temperature, but it is not easy to keep them healthy without extra light.

Pests and diseases: Generally trouble-free in the garden; susceptible to SPIDER MITES and VIRUS disease in the greenhouse.

Uses: Striking in beds and containers, alone or with other bedding plants. They combine well with browallia, sweet alyssum or lobelia.

Impatiens wallerana "common impatiens" BALSAMINACEAE
(Figure 2-6)

It is hard to find fault with impatiens, as they have so much to recommend them. They bloom from May to frost, even in heavy shade; they're easy to care for and are bothered by few pests and diseases; and they have attractive foliage and a compact habit of growth. The flowers are not spoiled by rain; there is no need to stake or deadhead; and they come in a wide (sometimes wild) color range and are adaptable to many uses in the garden. They will even pinch-hit on a sunny window sill for temporary color indoors. Not a bad repertoire!

The slightly iridescent, 2-inch (5-cm) flowers have five petals that overlap with the characteristic spur at the back of the flower. They come in shades of red, orange, rose, pale pink, white, mauve and striped combinations. The 2-inch (5-cm) leaves are dark green with scalloped edges.

Impatiens is a perennial in its native East Africa, but will not survive the frost. The seeds of impatiens, especially the excellent F_1 hybrid cultivars, are very expensive and the seedlings are slow-growing, which is why the price is often higher than that of other bedding plants. In recent years, there has been downward pressure on the price of bedding plants and some growers have stopped growing impatiens altogether. Some growers will cut corners by selling impatiens grown from cuttings, but such plants do not usually perform as well in the garden. You may be able to see the difference when shopping, because plants grown from cuttings tend to be thick at the base where they join the soil. Impatiens are not difficult to grow from seed; consider growing your own to take advantage of the wide selection in seed catalogues. Try the 'Super Elfin' series, 8–10 inches (20–25 cm); the 'Futura' series, 10–12 inches (25–30 cm); or the 'Twinkles' series if you like bicolors. The Park Seed Company catalogue lists cultivars for full sun.

Bloomtime: May to frost.

Height: 8–12 inches (20–30 cm), depending on the cultivar.

Light and soil: Light or full shade. They will take some sun, but not blazing hot sun all day. Impatiens like a light soil to which moist peat has been added, and benefit from a bit of bark mulch around their roots to keep them cool and moist.

How to grow: In mid-March, sow seeds and cover lightly with fine sterile sand. The seeds are as fine as dust, so you may find it easier to mix them with a spoonful of clean sand or sugar before sowing. Keep the soil temperature at 70°F (21°C) and cover the pots or flat with clear plastic until the seeds have germinated, about 16 days. Light and moisture are required for germination. When the seedlings are up, remove the plastic and grow on at 60–65°F (15–18°C). Do not overwater or overfertilize. Keep plants on the dry side for more compactness and bloom. Set plants out, 12 inches (30 cm) apart, at the end of May or early June. Fertilize with 20-20-20 monthly.

Pests and diseases: Generally trouble-free, although they may get APHIDS,

MITES or a PHYSIOLOGICAL CONDITION that causes premature leaf drop.
Uses: At the front of beds and mixed borders; in hanging baskets and planters, alone or with other bedding plants.

"Irish lace" see *Tagetes*
"Ivy, English" see *Hedera*
"Johnny-jump-up" see *Viola*
"Joseph's coat" see *Amaranthus*
"Kale, flowering or ornamental" see *Brassica*

Kochia scoparia forma *trichophylla* (*K. scoparia* var. *culta*) "summer cypress" "burning bush" CHENOPODIACEAE
(Figure 6-7)
Burning bush is so-named because it turns purplish-red in October, but in our wet climate it gets moldy and beaten down by fall rains before it turns red. Its other common name, summer cypress, gives a better idea of how it performs in our gardens. A half-hardy annual from southern Europe, it becomes a rounded ball of feathery bright green with tiny flowers. 'Childsii' has a more compact habit.
Bloomtime: Not grown for its blooms.
Height: 'Childsii' grows to 2 feet high by 1 foot wide (61 cm × 30 cm).
Light and soil: Full sun and a well-drained soil is best, but summer cypress will grow in all soils and light situations.
How to grow: Although young plants are not generally available from garden shops, they may be grown from seed sown indoors in March. Germinate at 60°F (15°C), harden off and set plants out in late May. Seeds can also be sown directly in the garden in April. Plants need support, as the rain water weighs them down in a wet summer.
Pests and diseases: Generally trouble-free.
Uses: Summer cypress makes an excellent dot plant for formal bedding, in the garden or in the center of a large container. It looks like a hedging plant and would make an effective temporary low hedge, to screen a part of the garden or set off a patio.

Lagurus see *Avena*

Lamiastrum galeobdolon '**Variegatum**' "silver nettle vine" LAMIACEAE
Like ivy and nepeta, silver nettle vine is added to hanging baskets for foliage interest. The creeping stems are square in cross-section and have a pair of leaves at 4-inch (10-cm) intervals. The leaves have scalloped edges,

with silver markings, flushed bronze in cold weather. It is hardy in the garden as a ground cover, but is quite invasive. Silver nettle vine is native to Europe.

Bloomtime: Grown for foliage rather than flowers, silver nettle vine may produce spikes of yellow flowers in June and July.

Height: Trailing to several feet (1 m).

Light and soil: Prefers some shade, but any soil will do.

How to grow: Young plants are generally available from shops in spring, or they can be started from cuttings taken at any time of year. Save plants from your hanging baskets at the end of the summer to reuse next spring. They will often survive in the container if left outdoors, or take the silver nettle vine out of the container, pot it up and tuck it in some warm corner of the garden where it will receive rain. The pot can be plunged into the garden soil and then lifted again in the spring; this is preferable to planting the vine directly into the ground, as it may invade the garden.

Pests and diseases: Generally trouble-free.

Uses: Trailing out of containers and from hanging baskets.

Lampranthus multiradiatus (*L. roseus, Mesembryanthemum multiradiatum, M. roseum*) "ice plant" "mesembryanthemum" AIZOACEAE

There are many plants which go by the common name ice plant, but this one is often sold in garden centers and planted in parks in the Pacific coast region. It has silky, shocking pink (rarely white), daisy-like flowers, to 1½ inches (4 cm) in diameter. Flowers usually open only on sunny days. The succulent gray-green leaves, to 1 inch (2.5 cm) long, are triangular in cross-section. Ice plant is a subshrub in its native South Africa, and may be overwintered indoors.

Just for information, the plant that grows along the highways in California, which is also called "ice plant," is *Carpobrotus* and is not grown here. The British refer to *Mesembryanthemum cristallinum* as ice plant because the leaves are covered with a sparkling coating which glistens in the sun. It is a South African plant which is rarely seen here.

Bloomtime: June to frost.

Height: Creeping plants, reaching up to 12 inches (30 cm) in height and spread.

Light and soil: Best in full sun and a hot spot. Ice plant requires well-drained, even dry, sandy soil. Too rich a soil will cause a lush growth of leaves but only a few flowers.

How to grow: Young plants are generally available from shops in spring, or they may be started from seed, available from Thompson and Morgan.

(T&M sell a mixture of *Lampranthus* species and hybrids, including orange and white.) Sow seeds at any time in the spring at a temperature of 70°F (21°C) and keep in the dark until seeds germinate (15–30 days). Transplant seedlings into individual pots when they are 1 inch (2.5 cm) high. Alternatively, take cuttings 2 inches (5 cm) long in late summer or early autumn. Remove lower leaves and leave cuttings to dry for a day before inserting them in pots of pure sand.

Pests and diseases: New shoots may be infested with APHIDS.

Uses: Excellent for hot dry places, especially rock gardens.

Lantana camara "lantana" VERBENACEAE
(Figure 7-7)

Lantana are somewhat of a specialty item. They really require a greenhouse for overwintering, but they are included here for general information. Lantana are usually seen in park plantings, where they are trained as standards, and can be up to 15 years old. The small flowers cluster in a rounded head at the end of the stems. With some cultivars, the flowers change color as they age, giving a fascinating rainbow effect. Shades include white, lilac, yellow, pink, rose and red, depending on the cultivar.

A shrub native to tropical America, lantana is a serious weed in some parts of the world. It has contaminated fields in South Africa and makes cattle ill. The foliage has quite a strong scent when touched, which some find offensive.

Bloomtime: May to October.

Height: 18–48 inches (46–122 cm) high by 36 inches (91 cm) wide. Trained as a standard, the trunk may be 5–6 feet (1.5–1.8 m) high.

Light and soil: Full sun and any rich, well-drained soil. Plants can either be grown in pots, which are easily moved in and out with the season, or they can be planted out in the spring and dug and brought into the greenhouse at the end of September.

How to grow: Young plants are sometimes available from shops in spring, or they can be started from 3-inch (7.5-cm) cuttings taken in August. Root in half peat/half sand with bottom heat. If plants are to be grown for bedding, pinch the tips to encourage bushiness. For standards, see instructions under *Fuchsia*, but train only one trunk up the stake. Lantana may also be grown from seed. Soak seeds 24 hours in warm water. Germination, at 70°F (21°C) soil temperature, takes about 1–3 months. Set hardened-off plants out in late May, spacing them 12 inches (30 cm) apart for bedding. At the end of September, bring them into the greenhouse and overwinter at 45°F (7°C), increasing temperature to 50–55°F (10–13°C) during March

97

and April. Plants will normally drop all their leaves. Keep them barely moist in winter and water them freely in spring and summer.

Pests and diseases: WHITEFLY is a pest in the greenhouse.

Uses: Standards make a lovely centerpiece to a formal bedding scheme. Used as bedding plants, lantana blooms tirelessly all summer and fall.

Lathyrus odoratus "sweet pea" FABACEAE
(Figure 3-5)

A hardy annual native to Italy, this sweet scented flower with its graceful blooms and soft colors has won many a gardener's heart. Most gardeners can find a corner in which to grow sweet peas; they are always welcome in a vase on the table or given in a bouquet.

The original sweet pea, which was deliciously fragrant, was a vine bearing small red and purple flowers. In 1699, a few seeds were sent from Father Francisco Cupani of Palermo to his friend Dr. Uvedale near London, England. Over the next two hundred years, English gardeners zealously selected sweet peas for flower size, ruffled petals and range of color, but unfortunately the scent was almost lost. Pizzetti and Cocker tell this story:

> "Charles Unwin, one of the major sweet pea hybridists of our time, . . . wrote that some years ago he received the gift of some Sweet Pea seeds from an almost forgotten English village. The flowers were small and not very attractive in color, but their fragrance was marvelous and, after an entire lifetime dedicated to Sweet Peas, Unwin admitted that, 'until that moment I never fully realized why Sweet Peas were so named'. Unfortunately, neither in England nor on the continent is it now possible to find seed of the original fragrant sweet peas. Possibly they *do* exist in some hidden out-of-the-way garden, and it would be a fascinating occupation to seek them out."

Seed of some very fragrant sweet peas may be acquired from the two English firms, Bolton and Unwin. Other seed catalogues also sell fragrant strains—look for names such as 'Old-fashioned' or 'Antique'. Sow a showy sweet pea and a fragrant sweet pea together, to get the best of both worlds.

There are hundreds of cultivars of sweet peas available in Britain, where there are sweet pea societies and shows devoted exclusively to sweet peas. All sweet peas will perform well in our mild climate. Dwarf cultivars that do not need staking are also available.

Bloomtime: June to frost if old flowers are removed and plants are well cared for.

Height: 1–6 feet (.3–1.8m), depending on the cultivar.

Light and soil: Bloom best in full sun with rich, well-drained soil that is neutral or slightly sweet. Add well-rotted manure or moist peat and some dolomite lime if necessary and dig well, preferably in autumn.

How to grow: Young plants are readily available from shops in spring, or they may be started from seed. As with most bedding plants, there is a much greater choice of cultivars when started from seed. In March, soak seeds for 24 hours to soften the seed coat, then sow and cover with ½ inch (1 cm) of potting mix. Germination, at 60°F (15°C) soil temperature, takes about 14 days. (Higher temperatures will inhibit germination.) Seeds may be sown directly in the garden in March, but they sometimes rot in a cold spring and are very easy to start indoors. A third method is to sow seeds directly in the garden in September or October, but the seedlings must be protected with a cloche through the winter. This gives excellent results in a mild winter. Pinch out the growing tips of young plants in February and remove the cloches in April.

Indoors, pinch the tips of seedlings when they are 4 inches (10 cm) high. Set hardened-off plants out in early May, spacing them 6–10 inches (15–25 cm) apart. Train tall-growing cultivars up canes or netting. Remove spent flowers and seed pods if any set. Feed every week with a half-strength 15-30-15 or similar fertilizer for best results.

Pests and diseases: SLUGS, APHIDS and SPIDER MITES may infest sweet peas. A number of fungi may cause problems, including root ROT (if seeded in a very cold, wet spring), POWDERY MILDEW, and GRAY MOLD. Mottling of the leaves and stunting may be caused by a VIRUS. That sounds frightening but, with the exception of root rot, these diseases are not common.

Uses: Use short types in the flower border, grow tall types at the back of the border on a trellis or in the middle of the border up a tripod of stakes. They can even be grown on a sunny balcony in a large container if the soil is rich and well watered. Sweet peas make excellent cut flowers.

Lavatera trimestris "lavatera" "mallow" MALVACEAE
(Figure 3-6)

The lavatera in public gardens always attracts attention and inspires creative guesswork as to its identity. Many people think it is some kind of petunia because of its trumpet-shaped flower. Others guess hollyhock (to which it is related) because of its upright growth habit. Lavatera is a very elegant hardy annual from the Mediterranean region, which deserves to be more widely grown. The 3-inch (7.5-cm) flowers have a distinctive pompon in the center of each trumpet. Plants are well-branched, with handsome rounded leaves that turn red in the fall.

The cultivar 'Mont Blanc' is glistening white and reaches 21 inches (53 cm) in height; 'Mont Rose' is pink and the same height; 'Loveliness' is pink but not as compact, reaching 3–4 feet (.9–1.2 m); 'Silver Cup', so named for winning the Fleuroselect Silver Cup, never before awarded to an annual, grows to 2 feet (.6 m) and has glowing, pink, 4-inch (10-cm) blooms.

Bloomtime: July to September.

Height: 21–48 inches (53–122 cm), depending on the cultivar.

Light and soil: Best in full sun and average, rather than rich, soil.

How to grow: In September or April, sow seeds where they are to bloom, just covering them with soil. Thin the seedlings to stand 12–18 inches (30–46 cm) apart. Alternatively, they may be started indoors in March in individual pots. Set hardened-off plants out in late May, spacing them 12–18 inches (30–46 cm) apart.

Pests and diseases: RUST may affect the leaves.

Uses: Use toward the center of a mixed border. May also be used for cutting.

Limonium sinuatum "statice" "sea lavender"
Psylliostachys suworowii (*Limonium suworowii, Statice suworowii*) "Russian statice" "rat-tail statice" PLUMBAGINACEAE
(Figure 2-7)

Although these two species are now in different genera, they are grouped together here because of their similarity, cultivation and use in the garden.

Common statice is a delightful plant from the Mediterranean that is easy to grow, attractive in the garden and provides everlasting flowers for arranging and art projects. The actual flowers are tiny and white, but each is surrounded by a tissue-paper-like calyx that keeps its bright color indefinitely. Colors include cream, rose, purple, blue and yellow. The flowers cluster at the top of long stems that have papery wings along them. The leaves, which are about 16 inches (41 cm) long, with deeply wavy margins, form a rosette around the base of the flower stems. Although statice is perennial in the wild, it is usually grown as an annual because it will not survive the frost. It is easy to grow from seed, which is available in separate colors or mixed colors.

Russian statice (closely related to common statice) is an annual native to southern USSR, Afghanistan and Iran. It has long pink flower spikes that stick up above the plant like pokers or twist around in corkscrew shapes. These striking flowers are excellent for fresh floral arrangements. The plants are similar in height and cultivation to the common statice.

Bloomtime: June to September.

Height: Most types grow 18–24 inches (46–61 cm); the dwarf cultivar of common statice, 'Petite Bouquet', reaches only 12 inches (30 cm).

Light and soil: Prefers full sun and any well-drained soil.

How to grow: Although young plants are not generally available from shops, they are easily grown from seed. In March, germinate at 60°F (15°C) soil temperature. Seeds of Russian statice may be slow to germinate. Set young plants out in May, spacing them 12 inches (30 cm) apart, closer for dwarf cultivars. Seeds may also be sown directly in the garden in May.

Pests and diseases: Generally trouble-free unless the summer is exceptionally damp, when the stems and flowers may get GRAY MOLD or POWDERY MILDEW.

Uses: Mixed borders, bedding schemes. Try dwarf types in mixed planters. Excellent dried (just hang in a cool dry place) for decorating wreaths and for arranging.

Lobelia erinus "edging lobelia" LOBELIACEAE
(Figures 6-8 and 8-6)

Lobelia is well-loved by gardeners for its deep rich shade of blue. This very dwarf spreader is native to South Africa, where it is a half-hardy annual or perennial, but it is generally grown as an annual in our climate. Lobelia has tiny flowers with three lower petals and two upper petals; some have a tiny spot of white at the throat. The flowers cover the plant in a mass of color, hiding the thin stems and small leaves. It was first introduced into European gardens in 1752, and now there are many beautiful cultivars. 'Mrs. Clibran' is blue with a white eye, 'White Lady' is white, 'Rosamund' is wine-red, 'Cambridge Blue' is light blue. All four have bright green leaves and reach about 8 inches (20 cm) in height. 'Crystal Palace' has dark blue flowers and bronzy foliage that intensifies the flower color. There are a number of cultivars that have a more trailing habit and are recommended for hanging baskets, but the dwarf types just mentioned trail enough to look good in hanging baskets. In fact, they often look better trailing out of mixed planters because they are neater than the trailing types.

Bloomtime: May to frost.

Height: 8 inches (20 cm), longer for trailing cultivars.

Light and soil: Lobelia will tolerate full sun if well-watered and it thrives in some shade. For best results, add some organic matter to the soil to retain moisture. If allowed to dry out, lobelia will turn brown and look wretched. I know more than one gardener (myself included) who has had to remove lobelia from hanging baskets after a lapse in watering. In the garden, a mulch of fir bark will keep plants cool and moist.

How to grow: Young plants are available from shops in spring, or they may be started from seed in late February. Sow several seeds in the center of a 3-inch (7.5-cm) pot, but do not cover. Germinate at 70°F (21°C) soil temperature for 21 days. Seedlings grow slowly. Plant the whole clump of seedlings out in lateMay, 4–8 inches (10–20 cm) apart. Because it is a perennial, rooted cuttings may be kept through winter in a sunny spot indoors. Stems usually root themselves along the ground as they grow; these rooted pieces can then be potted into sterilized soil.

Pests and diseases: Generally trouble-free, although seedlings may DAMP OFF.

Uses: Pattern plantings, edging of formal or mixed borders. Attractive in a more informal setting–under rhododendrons, for example. Outstanding in containers, either alone or with other bedding plants, and in hanging baskets with other bedding plants.

Lobularia maritima "sweet alyssum" "alyssum" BRASSICACEAE
(Figures 7-7 and 8-4)

Sweet alyssum, like ageratum, fibrous begonia, lobelia and marigold, is a most reliable and easy to grow summer bedding plant. From May to frost, it is a carpet of bloom, with dozens of tiny four-petalled flowers clustered at the tip of each spreading stem. Alyssum is available in white as 'Snow Crystals' (with larger flowers), 'Wonderland White', which stretches less (not such a problem in our cooler summers), 'Carpet of Snow' and 'Snow Cloth'. The Thompson and Morgan catalogue lists 'Sweet White', notable for its rich honey fragrance. There are a number of deep purple cultivars: 'Royal Carpet', 'Wonderland Deep Purple' and 'Navy Blue'. 'Wonderland Rosy-Red' and 'Rosie O'Day' are both rosy purple. Sweet alyssum is a perennial in its native Mediterranean region, but is grown as an annual here.

True alyssum, *Aurinia saxatile* (formerly *Alyssum saxatile*) is a winter-hardy perennial. It blooms earlier than the annual sweet alyssum, its cascading stems and sheets of bright yellow flowers a common sight in Pacific coast gardens. True alyssum is often seen growing with two other April-blooming perennials, *Iberis sempervirens* (the white evergreen candytuft) and *Aubrietia deltoides* (purple rock cress). These two species are often confused with purple and white sweet alyssum because of the similarity of their spreading habits.

Bloomtime: May to frost.

Height: 4 inches (10 cm) high.

Light and soil: More compact in full sun but tolerates some shade. Any well-drained soil. Tolerates drought and heat also.

How to grow: Young plants are generally available from shops in spring, or they may be started from seed sown in late March. Do not cover seeds, as light aids germination. Germinate at 60–70°F (15–21°C) soil temperature for 8 days. Grow on at 55–60°F (13–15°C). Set out hardened-off plants in May, spacing them 8 inches (20 cm) apart. Sweet alyssum will often seed itself in the garden; watch for the seedlings with their oval olive-green leaves when weeding in the spring. Plants may also be started by seeding them directly in the garden in April.

Pests and diseases: Indoors, seedlings may be susceptible to DAMPING-OFF. SLUGS like sweet alyssum and FLEA BEETLES may eat holes in the leaves of seedlings.

Uses: Pattern plantings and edging formal beds; at the front of mixed borders; in rock gardens and at the top of walls; in hanging baskets and in containers.

Lotus berthelotii "lotus vine" FABACEAE
(Figures 6-3 and 6-9)

Having just appeared on the market in the early eighties, lotus vine is fast gaining popularity for use in hanging baskets and containers. Its fine silvery foliage on long trailing branches sets off the blooms of other bedding plants. It is also striking in a hanging basket on its own. It blooms occasionally with red, 1-inch (2.5-cm), pea-like flowers.

Originally from the Canary Islands, it grows there as a shrub with trailing branches. It is not related to either the Egyptian water lotus (*Nymphaea lotus*) or the sacred lotus (*Nelumbo nucifera*), both water plants.

Bloomtime: Grown mainly for its foliage, but it does bloom occasionally.

Height: Trailing stems to 2 feet (.6 m) in length.

Light and soil: Full sun or part shade and any well-drained soil.

How to grow: Young plants should be purchased in shops in the spring, or cuttings can be made if you have access to a plant.

Pests and diseases: Watch for SPIDER MITES.

Uses: Trailing from hanging baskets and planters; cascading down a bank or in a rock garden. It can be pruned to keep it more compact.

"Love-in-a-mist" see *Nigella*
"Love-lies-bleeding" see *Amaranthus*

Lychnis coeli-rosa (*Silene coeli-rosa, Viscaria elegans*) "viscaria"
CARYOPHYLLACEAE
(Figure 2-8)

A confusion of botanical names exists around viscaria. There are many other species of *Silene* and *Lychnis*, so one must be careful to get the right one when ordering seeds or buying plants.

Viscaria has an airy quality, with 1-inch (2.5-cm) blooms atop wiry stems. Flowers come in shades of white, pink, mauve or rosy red. The leaves are long, narrow and gray-green. Long popular in England where it is a hardy annual, viscaria is being seen more often in our area, making a nice change in typical bedding plant arrangements.

Bloomtime: June to September.

Height: 6–18 inches (15–46 cm), depending on the cultivar.

Light and soil: Full sun or part shade and a well-drained soil.

How to grow: Although young plants are not generally available from shops, they are easily grown from seed. It is available from Thompson and Morgan, either through the catalogue, or from their seed racks in larger garden shops. Sow seeds indoors in March, germinating at a 60°F (15°C) soil temperature. Set out hardened-off plants in late May, spacing them 6 inches (15 cm) apart.

Pests and diseases: Generally trouble-free.

Uses: An elegant addition to the mixed border. Also attractive in containers and side-planted in moss baskets.

"Madagascar periwinkle" see *Catharanthus*
"Mallow" see *Lavatera*
"Maple, flowering" see *Abutilon*
"Marguerite, blue" see *Felicia*
"Marguerite daisy" see *Chrysanthemum frutescens*
"Marigold, African, French or signet" see *Tagetes*
"Marigold, Cape" see *Dimorphotheca*
"Marigold, English or pot" see *Calendula*
"Marvel-of-Peru" see *Mirabilis*
"Matricaria" see *Chrysanthemum parthenium*

Matthiola incana "stock" "common stock" BRASSICACEAE
(Figure 3-7)

A native of Europe, *Matthiola incana* was called "gillyflower" in the sixteenth century. In Shakespeare's *A Winter's Tale,* the shepherdess Perdita argues with the youth Polixenes over the merits of the striped gillyflowers. She says "of streak'd gillyvors. . . our rustic garden's barren, and I care not to get slips of them," explaining that she objects to man interfering with "great creating nature." This scene show us that even in the 1500s, gardeners were tinkering with plant selecting and knew how to propagate plants from cuttings (slips).

Although truly a hardy biennial, some stocks have been selected to bloom the first season from seed. 'Trisomic 7-Week' or '10-Week Mixed' are most commonly available in shops in spring. They produce bushy plants with upright stems bearing mostly double fragrant blooms. The color range includes white, pink, rose, crimson, dark blue and purple.

Some cultivars are "selectable" for doubleness. If seedlings are grown at 55–60°F (13–15°C), they will be two shades of green when at the two-leaf stage. Discard the dark green seedlings, because they will bear single flowers. This procedure is important to the British growers, who are very serious about stocks and have many tall cultivars suitable for exhibition and cutting. The latest development in selectable stocks–'Stockpot'–comes from Japan. They have bred stock seedlings to have a notch on the leaf if they are going to be double. Seedlings without the notch can be thrown out.

I'm sure commercial bedding plant growers don't select for doubleness, but you certainly could if you grew your own seedlings. Double stocks are formal in style, single stocks are more informal–perfect for a natural setting where they can be allowed to seed themselves. Figure 3-7 shows both double and single flowers.

Bloomtime: June and July from March sowings, August and September from May sowings.

Height: 1–3 feet (.3–.9 m), depending on the cultivar.

Light and soil: Prefers full sun, but will tolerate some shade. A rich, well-drained soil to which some dolomite lime and organic matter has been added is best.

How to grow: Young plants are sometimes available from shops in spring, or they may be started from seed sown March to May. Germinate for 14 days at 70°F (21°C). Grow on at 50–55°F (10–13°C). (See note about selecting for doubles above.) Do not allow seedlings to be damaged or dry out, as they will bloom poorly. Handle seedlings by their leaves rather than their stems and do not overwater, to reduce the possibility of infection by damping-off fungi. Plant out from late April on, 12 inches (30 cm) apart. For a later bloom, sow directly in the garden.

Pests and diseases: In the insect department, watch for FLEA BEETLES, CATERPILLARS and APHIDS. Like other members of the cabbage family, stocks may be afflicted by CLUB ROOT. Other fungal diseases include DAMPING-OFF, basal and root ROTS and MOLDS. Although this sounds discouraging, stocks are easy to grow.

Uses: A fragrant addition to beds, borders, bouquets and floral decorations.

Matthiola longipetala subsp. *bicornis* "evening scented stock" "night scented stock" BRASSICACEAE

Evening scented stock is not much to look at, with narrow gray-green leaves, up to 2 inches (5 cm) long, and tiny pink or mauve flowers spaced along thin flower stalks. It will hardly be noticed among the other plants except for its fragrance filling the air in the evening and on dull days. It is easy to grow—a packet of seeds scattered into a flower bed or planter near a door or window is an inspired addition to the garden.

Evening scented stock is native to Greece. The name *bicornis* means "two-horns," and refers to the two horn-like structures at the end of the ¾-inch (2-cm) seed capsules.

Bloomtime: Evening scented stock begins blooming about two months after sowing, continuing for two months.

Height: 12 inches (30 cm).

Light and soil: Prefers full sun but will tolerate some shade. Plant in any well-drained soil to which some organic matter has been added.

How to grow: Rarely available as plants in shops, but easy to grow from seed. Sow seeds directly in the garden in April and again mid-May and late June to get flowers all summer.

Pests and diseases: Generally trouble-free.

Uses: To add fragrance to the garden or hanging baskets.

"Mesembryanthemum" see *Cleretum* and *Lampranthus*

Mimulus **hybrids** "monkey flower" "mimulus" SCROPHULARIACEAE
(Figure 1-9)

Monkey flowers are one of the few annuals that do well in shade and wet soil. There are several parent species of monkey flower, native to swampy areas of North and South America; some are perennials and some annuals. Monkey flowers are generally grown as annuals, as they will not survive the frost.

106

The showy, 1- to 2-inch (2.5- to 5-cm) flowers, in bright yellow, orange and red shades, often have spots on the petals. They aren't easy to combine with other flowers, but are certainly colorful enough to make a show on their own.

Bloomtime: May to August.

Height: 12 inches (30 cm).

Light and soil: Shade to sun, with a moist soil.

How to grow: Young plants are generally available from shops in spring, or they may be started from seed. Sow seeds indoors in March, but do not cover with soil, as light is required for germination. Cover flats or pots with clear plastic or glass to maintain humidity. Germination, at 60–70°F (15–21°C) soil temperature, takes about 10 days. Set out hardened-off plants in late May, spacing them 8 inches (20 cm) apart.

Pests and diseases: Generally trouble-free.

Uses: So showy they may be best on their own, or with yellow or rust-colored flowers. Use in beds and containers.

Mirabilis jalapa "four-o'clock" "marvel-of-Peru" NYCTAGINACEAE

A bushy plant with large coarse leaves, *Mirabilis* bears dozens of trumpet-shaped blooms about 1 inch (2.5 cm) in diameter. They can be red, yellow, orange, rose or white; they are sometimes striped and often have more than one flower color on a single plant, making a very pretty effect. The only drawback to four-o'clocks is that the flowers are only open early in the morning, on dull days and late in the day—hence the name. (Actually, they should be called five o'clocks due to daylight saving time.) They have large seeds that germinate quickly and produce large seedlings, making them an ideal plant for a child's garden. The other common name refers to their origin, Peru, where they are perennial. They form a tuberous root that can be taken up and stored through the winter, like a dahlia, to be set out again in spring.

Bloomtime: July to frost.

Height: 2 feet (.6 m).

Light and soil: Prefers full sun and any well-drained soil, but might be worth trying afternoon shade to see more bloom. They will do well in very sandy soil and in hot windy places, but like an abundance of water in the summer.

How to grow: Sow seeds in the garden in April, or indoors in March. The big seeds are easy for a young child to handle. Plant seedlings outdoors in May, 12 inches (30 cm) apart. Before the first frost, dig up the tuberous roots, let them dry and store them in a box of peat in a cool, dark place.

Plant them out again in April.

Pests and diseases: APHIDS may infest growing tips.

Uses: In mixed borders and in large containers. Best in an informal setting, rather than formal bedding schemes.

Moluccella laevis "bells of Ireland" LAMIACEAE
(Figure 8-5)

This unusual plant, a half-hardy annual native to Asia Minor, is fun to grow. Each node on the stem produces two scalloped leaves and a cluster of seven or eight lime-green "bells" that encircle the stem, facing outward. Each bell is actually the calyx of a flower and a single stem will bear flowers at various stages. Near the top of the stem, the bells will contain a fuzzy white unopened flower bud, further down a tiny white flower and below that the flowers will have fallen off, leaving just the calyx. As the plant grows, the stems full of bells become over 1 foot (30 cm) long and make an interesting addition to a flower border and outstanding cut flowers, lasting well over a week. (Pick off the two leaves at each node, as they detract from the bells.)

Bloomtime: Grown for the green, bell-like calyces, which appear with the flowers from June to September.

Height: To 3 feet (.9 m). Stake bells of Ireland to produce long straight stems or use the curving stems in asymmetrical flower arrangements.

Light and soil: Prefer full sun and any well-drained soil. They will give even better results if some organic matter is added to the soil.

How to grow: Although young plants are not generally available from shops, they may be grown from seed. In March, refrigerate seeds for 5 days before sowing indoors in sandy soil. Germination is irregular, occurring over a 5-week period. Alternating soil temperature between 50°F (10°C) at night and 70°F (21°C) in the day encourages germination. Harden off and plant out 9 inches (23 cm) apart in May. Seeds may also be sown directly in the garden in April and thinned. Many books say the seedlings are difficult to transplant into the garden, but this has not been my experience. Stake plants with light bamboo canes.

Pests and diseases: Generally trouble-free.

Uses: In a mixed border or large planter; excellent for cut flowers. They may be dried (most successfully with silica gel).

"Monkey flower" see *Mimulus*
"Moss rose" see *Portulaca*

Myosotis sylvatica "forget-me-not" BORAGINACEAE

Forget-me-nots are low-growing, spreading plants with small, sky blue flowers, each with a white eye. Biennials by nature, young forget-me-nots are planted in the fall, along with bulbs, to bloom the following spring. Once in the garden, they seed themselves and may easily be moved. The seedlings are simple to identify because they have hairy, bright green leaves that are broad across the middle and taper to each end. The leaves grow in a rosette shape, joined at the base. It is not until their second year that the flowering stems are produced and their ultimate height is reached.

The name *Myosotis* comes from the Greek meaning "mouse ear," no doubt because of the fuzziness of the leaves rather than their shape. There is some confusion of the names in this genus. Seed catalogues often list forget-me-nots as *Myosotis alpestris*, a name correctly applied to a perennial that is rarely known in cultivation. *Myosotis scorpioides* (or *M. palustris*) is the water forget-me-not, a creeping bog plant.

There are many sentimental stories about the origin of the common name. In their marvelous book *Flowers: A Guide for Your Garden*, Pizzetti and Cocker tell us:

"The most pleasing and simplest story has for its protagonists the forget-me-not and God, who, according to the German tradition of this legend, is an old, very dignified, melancholy figure. . . . After much work distributing names among all the animals, plants, flowers and objects, a small voice cried out 'Forget me not, O Lord,' and God replied, 'Forget-me-not shall be your name.' And so it has been."

Forget-me-nots are also available in pink and white.

Bloomtime: March to May.

Height: 8–24 inches (20–61 cm), depending on the cultivar. Most garden cultivars are under 12 inches (30 cm).

Light and soil: Sun or shade and any well-drained soil, preferably one to which some organic matter has been added.

How to grow: Young plants are generally available from shops in spring or fall; sometimes they are in the perennial section. However, they are easy to grow from seed. During summer, sow seeds where they are to bloom or in an out-of-the-way bed for transplanting in autumn. Space seedlings 6 inches (15 cm) apart. Plants will bloom the following spring.

Pests and diseases: In very wet weather, plants may get MILDEW or MOLD.

Uses: Use as a "winter bedding plant": planted in fall to bloom in early spring. Attractive planted at the front of a mixed border or under roses. Use in containers with spring bloomers.

"Nasturtium" see *Tropaeolum*

Nemesia strumosa "nemesia" SCROPHULARIACEAE
(Figure 1-10)
A charming half-hardy annual from South Africa, nemesia is well suited to our climate, for it doesn't grow well where the weather is too hot or humid. The flowers, to 1 inch (2.5 cm) across, are white, orange, yellow, pink or lilac, some with spots on the outer petals or in the bearded throat. The colors are fresh, but not too intense. The plants are erect and well-branched, with long, narrow, light green leaves.
Bloomtime: June to August, when they can be cut back to flower a second time. Bloomtime can also be extended by making a second sowing.
Height: 8–12 inches (20–30 cm), depending on the cultivar.
Light and soil: Full sun to shade in a soil with lots of organic matter. Any stress will result in spindly plants, so keep them well-fertilized and watered.
How to grow: Young plants are generally available from shops in spring, or they can be started from seed in March. Germinate in the dark at 60°F (15°C) for 7–14 days. Set out hardened-off plants, 4–6 inches (10–15 cm) apart, in May. A second sowing can be made in May for later summer bloom.
Pests and diseases: If soil is too cold or wet, plants can suffer root ROT.
Uses: Lovely in hanging baskets, beds and containers for early summer color. Try planting with browallia or cupflower, which are slow to get going but have a strong finish. They can take over from the nemesia.

Nemophila menziesii (*N. insignis*) "baby blue eyes" HYDROPHYLLACEAE
(Figure 2-9)
This hardy annual from California has a bright and cheerful effect in the garden. The sky blue flowers have five overlapping petals and a white center, set off by fresh green leaves. The habit is open and sprawling, which makes baby blue eyes more suited to a rockery, or trailing out of a container with other bedding plants, than a formal bedding plant scheme. The specific name honors Archibald Menzies, a British Royal Navy surgeon. He joined Captain George Vancouver's voyage to the Pacific coast in 1792 in order to collect botanical specimens for King George III's "very valuable

collection of exotics at Kew [gardens]"–Vancouver's own words.
Bloomtime: June to September.
Height: 6–8 inches (15–20 cm), spreading to over 12 inches (30 cm) across.
Light and soil: Full sun or light shade, well-drained soil, preferably with added organic matter. Water well in summer.
How to grow: Sow seeds in March, either indoors or in their garden locations. Many books say the seedlings are difficult to transplant into the garden, but this has not been my experience. Plants should be spaced about 9 inches (23 cm) apart. Stems are quite brittle, so take care when weeding around baby blue eyes. They do not seem to mind a bit of bark mulch around their roots to keep them cool and moist.
Pests and diseases: APHIDS may infest new shoots.
Uses: Rock gardens, informal woodland settings, trailing out of containers.

"Nepeta" see *Glechoma*

Nicotiana alata "flowering tobacco" "nicotiana" SOLANACEAE
(Figure 8-7)

Although related to the tobacco plant, *Nicotiana alata* is grown only for decorative value. Like its cousin, it has large handsome leaves that grow up to 12 inches (30 cm) long and are diamond-shaped in outline. The flowers consist of a long tube opening out into a star shape 2 inches (5 cm) across. They are very elegant, in shades of white, pink, rose, red or dusky purple, and, in some cultivars, are fragrant. Flowers of the parent species close during the day, but those of the cultivars remain open all day. Plants can grow up to 5 feet (1.5 m) tall, making the dwarf cultivars more suitable to most gardens. The 'Nicki' series, most common in shops, reach 16–18 inches (41–46 cm) and are not fragrant. 'Lime Green' reaches 30 inches (76 cm) and has an unusual flower color that is striking in floral arrangements. The 'Domino' series grows to 12–14 inches (30–36 cm) and plants are bushier, producing more flowers. They come in separate colors or a mix, which, depending on the seed house, includes lime green. Native to South America where it is perennial, flowering tobacco likes warmth and will not survive winters outdoors in the Pacific coast region.
Bloomtime: June to frost.
Height: 1–5 feet (.3–1.5 m), depending on the cultivar.
Light and soil: Full sun or part shade and a rich, well-drained soil to which much organic matter has been added.
How to grow: Young plants are generally available from shops in spring, or

they can easily be grown from seed. Sow seeds indoors in March, but do not cover with soil, as light is required for germination, which, at 70°F (21°C) soil temperature, takes about 14 days. Set out hardened off plants 12 inches (30 cm) apart when the weather has warmed up, late May or early June.

Pests and diseases: Young plants may be infested with APHIDS.

Uses: Dwarf cultivars in containers, mixed beds and borders, and for cutting.

Nierembergia hippomanica var. *violacea* *(N. caerulea)* "cupflower"
SOLANACEAE
(Figure 5-8)

Cupflower belongs to the same family as flowering tobacco and petunias and is also native to South America. Perennial in its homeland, it is grown as a half-hardy annual in the Pacific coast region. The foliage is attractive: finely cut, dark green and feathery. The plant forms a mound about 1 foot (30 cm) high and wide. In June there is a scattering of bloom, but by later in the summer the plants are almost covered with 1-inch (2.5-cm), violet-purple, cup-shaped flowers. Plants that have been grown from cuttings may bloom more heavily earlier in the summer.

Bloomtime: June to frost.

Height: 12 inches (30 cm).

Light and soil: Prefers full sun and any well-drained soil.

How to grow: Young plants are not generally available from shops, but they are easily grown from seed. Sow seeds indoors in March, germinating at 60°F (15°C). Set young plants out, spaced 8 inches (20 cm) apart, in late May or June. Plants can also be started from cuttings taken in late summer, rooted in a sandy soil mix, and overwintered in the greenhouse. Cupflower is borderline hardy near the Pacific coast and may survive a mild winter, particularly if it is taken into a more protected place, such as a garage, or protected under cloches.

Pests and diseases: Generally trouble-free.

Uses: Excellent as an edging to a flower bed or mixed border, particularly from August on when the bloom is most abundant. Also suitable for rock gardens, containers and hanging baskets.

Nigella damascena "love-in-a-mist" "nigella" RANUNCULACEAE
(Figure 2-10)

Love-in-a-mist is an oddball annual like bells of Ireland, and just as easy to grow. The finely cut leaves create a green "mist" that surrounds the delicate white or blue flowers. The flowers of most cultivars have a double row of papery petals and resemble cornflowers. They are excellent cut flowers and produce an interesting round seed capsule that dries well and can be used for flower arrangements.

Love-in-a-mist gets its botanical name from the Latin *niger*, meaning black. This refers to its tiny jet-black seeds, which look like chips of coal. They can be saved and will be viable for up to two years.

Love-in-a-mist has been known since ancient times, when it was valued for its medicinal properties. Native to Asia Minor, it also grows wild in the Mediterranean.

Bloomtime: June to August, longer if a second sowing is made.

Height: 18 inches (46 cm) or more.

Light and soil: Prefers full sun and any well-drained soil with added organic matter.

How to grow: Although young plants are not generally available from shops, they are easily grown from seed. Many books say the seedlings are difficult to transplant into the garden, but this has not been my experience. Sow seeds in the garden or indoors in March, just covering them with soil. Young plants should be spaced 9 inches (23 cm) apart. Dry seed pods by hanging them upside-down in a cool, dry place.

Pests and diseases: Generally trouble-free.

Uses: Wonderful for a soft textural effect in a mixed border. Good for cutting and drying.

Osteospermum ecklonis (*Dimorphotheca ecklonis*) "African daisy" "osteospermum" ASTERACEAE
(Figure 8-8)

This particular African daisy—as other plants go by the same name—is a subshrub from southern Africa. It has daisy-like flowers up to 3 inches (7.5 cm) with white petals and a striking navy blue disk at the center. The plant has a bushy habit, similar to that of a marguerite, and handsome dark green foliage. There are many more species of osteospermum growing in South Africa which may find their way into gardens in years to come. Young plants of *Osteospermum ecklonis* are sometimes sold as Spanish marguerite, which is strange since they are from Africa.

Bloomtime: June to frost. Remove old flowers to encourage continued bloom.

Height: To 24 inches (61 cm) high.

113

Light and soil: Prefers full sun, a hot spot and any well-drained soil.

How to grow: Young plants grown from cuttings are sometimes available from shops in spring, or make cuttings yourself if you have access to a plant. Set plants out in late May, 12 inches (30 cm) apart. Remove old flowers for continued bloom.

Pests and diseases: In a very wet, cold summer, GRAY MOLD may develop on the leaves.

Uses: Very striking in a mixed border or in a large planter with other bedding plants. Try them combined with lavender and felicia.

"Painted-tongue" see *Salpiglossis*
"Pansy," "tufted pansy" see *Viola*

Papaver nudicaule "Iceland poppy" PAPAVERACEAE
(Figure 7-8)

This native of the subarctic is a short-lived perennial, usually grown as a biennial or hardy annual. The leaves form a rosette around the base of the plant, which throws up 18- to 24-inch (46- to 61-cm) stems with 2- to 4-inch (5- to 10-cm) fragrant blooms of orange, yellow, apricot, white, pink, scarlet or rose. 'Champagne Bubbles' has pastel blooms on 24-inch (61-cm) stems, making excellent cut flowers; 'Sparkling Bubbles' has deeper shades; 'Garden Gnome' and 'Wonderland' are dwarf cultivars, suitable for bedding or rockery schemes.

Bloomtime: June to September.

Height: 10–24 inches (25–61 cm), depending on the cultivar.

Light and soil: Prefers full sun and any well-drained soil. Poor, dry soils are more suitable than rich, damp soils.

How to grow: Young plants are sometimes available from shops in spring, or they can easily be grown from seed. Sow indoors in March or April, transplanting them when young into individual pots. (Plants develop a tap root and resent root disturbance.) Another method, as they are hardy annuals, is to sow them directly in the garden in March, just covering them with soil. Plants should be spaced to stand 8–10 inches (20–25 cm) apart. Remove faded flowers.

Pests and diseases: In wet, cold summers the leaves may get POWDERY MILDEW.

Uses: In addition to bedding, borders and rock gardens, Iceland poppies make excellent cut flowers. Cut stems in the morning, just as the nodding buds are lifting but before the flowers open. Sear stems in boiling water or with a flame.

Papaver rhoeas selections "Shirley poppy" PAPAVERACEAE
"In Flanders' fields the poppies blow,
Between the crosses, row on row. . . "
These lines, written by John McRae in 1915, have immortalized the humble
weed *Papaver rhoeas*, the corn or field poppy and inspired the small, felt
poppies worn around the world on Remembrance Day.

A hardy annual native to vast areas of Europe and Asia, field poppies
have erect, slender stems covered with minute, silky hairs. The nodding
bud opens to reveal a blood-red flower, 2 inches (5 cm) in diameter, like
crushed silk. The leaves are about 6 inches (15 cm) long, covered with
small hairs and divided. This species, with *Papaver somniferum* (opium
poppy), produce the commercial poppy seed used in cooking.

Pizzetti and Cocker relate the story of the creation of the Shirley poppies
from an account written by their originator, the Reverend W. Wilks:

"In 1880 I noticed in an abandoned corner of my garden a group of
the common red poppy, *Papaver rhoeas*, among which was a solitary
flower with petals slightly margined in white. I marked the flower and
saved the seed, which the following year produced about two hundred plants, four or five of which had white edged petals. The best of
these were marked, their seed saved, and the same process of selection and elimination was repeated for several years; with the subsequent flowers having an increasingly large area of white on the petals and correspondingly smaller areas of red until a pale pink form
was obtained, followed by a plant with white flowers. Next I began
the long process of changing the centers of the flowers from black to
yellow, and then to white, until I succeeded in obtaining a group of
plants with petals ranging in color from brilliant red to pure white,
with all the intermediate shades of pink plus an extensive selection
with margined and suffused petals; all the flowers having yellow or
white stamens, anthers and pollen, and a white center. . . It is interesting to note that all the gardens of the world, whether they be rich
or poor, are ornamented by direct descendents of the single seed capsule cultivated in the vicarage garden at Shirley [England] during the
August of 1880."

Reverend Wilks had reason to be proud of his creation, as they are ex-
quisite flowers. There are also double Shirley poppies available and
Thompson and Morgan list 'Rev. Wilks Mixed' as having many fancy types
such as bicolors and picotees. 'Allegro' is a dwarf field poppy of the original

type; the Stokes catalogue suggests planting them near graves for remembrance as well as borders and rock gardens.

Bloomtime: June to August.

Height: 12–36 inches (30–91 cm), depending on the cultivar.

Light and soil: The same as *Papaver nudicaule*.

How to grow: See *Papaver nudicaule*.

Pests and diseases: See *Papaver nudicaule*.

Uses: In mixed borders and informal gardens. Good in containers with other bedding plants so that their delicate flowers can be viewed at close range.

Pelargonium x*domesticum* "regal pelargonium" "Martha Washington geranium" "pansy geranium" "pelargonium" GERANIACEAE
(Figure 8-9)

Like the zonal geraniums, regal pelargoniums are the result of complex plant breeding, mainly derived from three species: *P. cucullatum, P. fulgidum,* and *P. grandiflorum*, all half-hardy perennials from South Africa. The flowers are more delicate than those of the zonals; in shades of peach, pink, bronze, lavender, white and red, they often have petal edges or throats of a contrasting color. The foliage is a brighter green and has pointed teeth along the leaf margin, rather than the more scalloped edges of the zonals. The leaves do not have the dark rings that characterize the zonal geraniums. All four common names are in use, but pelargonium is preferred by Europeans and Martha Washington geranium is used more by Americans.

Bloomtime: May to October.

Height: 15–24 inches (38–61 cm), depending on the cultivar.

Light and soil: The same as zonal geraniums (*Pelargonium* x*hortorum*).

How to grow: Regal pelargoniums are always grown from cuttings of named cultivars and sold in bloom in shops in spring. The flowers are damaged by rain, so they are best grown on a covered patio or on an apartment balcony, for example. Cuttings can be taken from plants in September, but whitefly is a problem, particularly for regal pelargoniums indoors.

Pests and diseases: WHITEFLY.

Uses: Best in containers on a covered balcony or patio.

Pelargonium x*hortorum* "geranium" "zonal geranium" "zonal pelargonium" GERANIACEAE
(Figures 6-3, 6-10, 7-7, 8-3, 8-6 and 8-10)

To the home gardener, there is no doubt that the summer bedding plants

116

with vivid red flowers, large rounded leaves and a characteristic pungent odor are geraniums. Correctly, however, they are in the genus *Pelargonium*, and there is a movement in gardening circles to use pelargonium as a common name to distinguish them from true geraniums. True geraniums (in the genus *Geranium*) are frost-hardy perennials with small flowers in pastel shades.

Because the name geranium has been used so extensively for the past two hundred years to describe *Pelargonium xhortorum*, there is something to be said for continuing to use it. Even the color "geranium red" is commonly used.

Most gardening magazines and catalogues use geranium. A number of gardening books, particularly those from Britain, prefer pelargonium. Most gardeners continue to use geranium to refer to the summer bedding plant, using true geranium or hardy geranium when meaning plants in the genus *Geranium*. Unlike use of botanical names, there is no one correct common name. In this book, the popular use of geranium is retained.

The first zonal geraniums were sent to Holland from South Africa in 1609 by the governor of the Cape colony. During the late 1700s and the early 1800s, the Cape colony passed into British hands and at the same time there was a boom in greenhouse growing in Britain. Many species of *Pelargonium* were imported into Britain and their popularity peaked in the Victorian era. During World War I, growing ornamental plants in greenhouses in Britain was banned due to fuel shortages, and geranium numbers fell.

In the 1950s and '60s in America, disease was a tremendous problem with geraniums, wiping out vast crops. The culprits were the fungal disease verticillium wilt, bacterial blight and a number of viral diseases. The advent of Culture-Virus-Indexing has completely changed the situation, allowing disease-free plants to be grown. This a technique whereby plants are grown in a laboratory until they are free of disease organisms and new plants are raised from this "clean" stock. In addition, from years of patient breeding, the British, Dutch and Americans have developed thousands of cultivars, including all the "fancy leaf geraniums."

In addition to the typical red, geranium flower colors include pale pink, hot pink, salmon, white and orange. Leaves often have a circle of darker green on them, the "zone" for which they are named. Fancy leaf cultivars include green and white or green and gold leaves, or solid yellow leaves and hundreds of other combinations. Many of these fancy cultivars are named clones, and must be propagated by cuttings and overwintered. Plants are available from specialty growers or clubs.

Plant hybridizers have produced many cultivars that can be grown from seed. If you look closely at the plants for sale in the shops in spring, you can generally spot those that have been grown from seed. They are usually sold in rectangular packs of thin plastic, with 24 individual plants to a flat. Geraniums from cuttings are usually sold in at least 4-inch (10-cm) pots. They have larger leaves and the stem is fairly thick where it meets the soil.

An important difference between geraniums grown from seed and cuttings is the time at which they will begin to bloom. Geraniums grown from cuttings are usually in bud or bloom by April or May. Seed geraniums may or may not be, depending on when they were seeded and whether the grower gave the seedlings additional light. When buying seed geraniums, look for good-sized plants with flower buds. Immature seedlings will not produce bloom until July or August.

There are four main advantages to the seed-grown geraniums: plants are usually disease-free (diseases can be transferred when cuttings are taken), they develop a symmetrical growth habit, they produce more flowers and they are less expensive. Outstanding seed cultivars include the Fleuroselect-winning 'Sprinter Series', AAS winner 'Rose Diamond', Fleuroselect winner 'Cherry Diamond' and 'Scarlet Diamond'.

Bloomtime: May until frost (July or August until frost for seed geraniums, depending on how they were raised).

Height: Usually 1–3 feet (.3–.9 m), but if they are trained up a stake and overwintered in a greenhouse, they may reach up to 6 feet (1.8 m).

Light and soil: Although most zonal geraniums prefer full sun, some of the cultivars with golden leaves may burn in full sun. Zonal geraniums may also burn in a very hot place, such as a hot greenhouse or a spot that has a lot of reflected light and trapped heat. Any well-drained soil is fine; they tolerate dry soil.

How to grow: Young plants are always available from shops in spring or they can be started from seed, but it is a slow process. They take six months from sowing to blooming. In December or January, soak seeds between two wet paper towels for 48 hours, then sow ¼ inch (.6 cm) apart and cover with ⅛ inch (.3 cm) of fine potting soil. Cover flat with clear plastic for 5 days and maintain 70°F (21°C) soil temperature; germination takes 12–25 days. Transplant when the first true leaves appear and keep soil temperature at 70°F (21°C) during the day, but 60°F (15°C) during the night, to keep plants compact. Use artificial lights for 18 hours each day, beginning when seeds germinate and continuing for six weeks to produce bloom in May or early June.

The following technique is used with good results in Britain and reduces energy consumption in the greenhouse. Seeds are sown at the beginning of October, and soil temperature is kept at least 70°F (21°C) until seeds germinate. The temperature is then reduced to 65°F (18°C) until transplanting, when it is further reduced to 45°F (7°C). Using this technique, plants bloom about the last week of May.

Set hardened-off plants out in late May, 12 inches (30 cm) apart. Best long-term results will be obtained by removing flowers and buds when setting the plants out. Flower stalks snap off easily from where they join the main stem. Through the summer, remove old flowers and dead or yellow leaves and pinch back the growing tip from time to time. (The growing tip is where the new leaves are unfurling. Often you will see a tiny flower bud just beside them. If you are careful, it is possible to pinch just the leaves, not disturbing the flower bud.)

In September, cuttings can be taken to be overwintered indoors. Using a razor blade, take 3- to 4-inch (7.5- to 10-cm) cuttings from healthy plants. Carefully remove all leaves from the bottom inch (2.5 cm) of the cutting. Fill 2¼-inch (6-cm) pots (or styrofoam cups with a hole in the bottom) with a moist rooting mix of ⅔ perlite and ⅓ peat, and make a hole in the mix with a dibble or pencil. Insert one cutting to each pot. Roots should appear in 7–10 days, at which time cuttings should be potted into 4-inch (10-cm) pots with a good potting mix. Fertilize with half-strength 20-20-20 once a month until March. If plants are in a warm greenhouse and are growing quickly, they can be fertilized more often. Pinch tips when about 6 inches (15 cm) high.

Zonal geraniums bloom best with a restricted root zone, so do not plant them into a too large container. In Europe, some gardeners prefer to keep plants in their pots all summer, plunging the pots into the soil. This also has the advantage of keeping the roots drier and more compact, a benefit in wet soils. Eight-inch (20-cm) pots are adequate for this technique.

Various techniques are used for overwintering geranium plants. Some gardeners dig plants up, shake the soil off, and hang them upside down. Other gardeners dig plants up and pot them into boxes of soil. In both cases they should be placed in a cool, frost-free place, such as a garage. The ideal temperature is about 50°F (10°C). A third method is to pot plants up in sterilized potting mix, cut them back by one-third and keep them in a sunny window in the house through the winter.

Pests and diseases: GRAY MOLD causes gray fuzzy patches on stems and leaves. In the greenhouse, WHITEFLIES and LEAFHOPPERS may be a problem. VIRUS diseases can be carried between plants by APHIDS and LEAFHOPPERS; they can be spread by tools when cuttings are made.

Whether you buy seedlings or rooted cuttings, do not buy plants with leaves that are puckered or crinkled or with round yellow rings on them, signs of viral disease.

There are a few PHYSIOLOGICAL DISORDERS which indicate a cultural problem. In general, these disorders are temporary and when the weather warms up, the symptoms disappear. If plants appear to be healthy otherwise, they are not cause for concern. OEDEMA is caused in the greenhouse by moist soil in combination with cool, cloudy spring weather. The plants take up too much water and "water blisters" form on the undersides of the leaves. They burst and then form cork-like spots. Although unsightly, this condition disappears when the weather warms. LEAF REDDENING occurs if the nights are too cool in the greenhouse; again, it's not a problem once the plants are set out. Dry soil will cause DRY BROWN PATCHES on the leaves. In itself this is not a problem on one or two leaves, but it can indicate that the plants have not been properly cared for.

Uses: Excellent for bedding schemes and edging and a must for containers, zonal geraniums combine well with many other bedding plants. Consider them behind sweet alyssum or dusty miller, interplanted with heliotrope or felicia, or with marigolds or calendula, if you are partial to bright colors. They work well with marguerite daisies, especially 'Silver Lace'. Zonal geraniums look great with blue lobelia and silvery lotus vine, trailing from a large planter. A classic is a large zonal geranium (or several) in a heavy terra cotta pot.

Pelargonium peltatum "ivy geranium" "trailing geranium" GERANIACEAE (Figure 3-8)

Ivy geraniums are beautifully suited to hanging basket and container cultivation. Blooms, some double, are in shades of pink, white, crimson and mauve. The leaves, as the common name suggests, resemble ivy leaves in shape, but are bright green. Like the other pelargoniums, ivy geraniums are native to South Africa, but they do not like full sun and burn easily. The vast majority of the plants sold in shops are named cultivars grown from cuttings, but there is a new seed mixture, 'Summer Showers', which has gotten excellent comments by gardeners. An interesting group of cultivars, the Swiss balcony geraniums or mini-cascade geraniums, are much more floriferous than the common ivy geraniums. Although they begin to bloom a bit later and have smaller flowers, they become a mass of bloom trailing 2 feet (1.2 m) from a window box, even on the north side of a house. Flowers are "self-cleaning," and do not need to be deadheaded.

Bloomtime: May to frost.

Height: Trailing to 18–24 inches (46–61 cm), depending on the cultivar.
Light and soil: Full or partial shade and well-drained soil with added organic matter. Too much sun will result in small, cup-shaped leaves and small blooms with some burning.
How to grow: Young plants are almost always available from shops in spring, or they can be started from cuttings or seed as for zonal geraniums, except that plants must be kept more shaded.
Pests and diseases: See *Pelargonium* x*domesticum*. Ivy geraniums are most susceptible to OEDEMA, so water only in the morning and on sunny days. Keep well fertilized.
Uses: Hanging baskets, either alone or with other bedding plants; trailing over the edge of containers or walls.

Petunia x*hybrida* "petunia" SOLANACEAE
(Figure 5-9)
For all-summer and autumn bloom in the widest range of colors imaginable, it is hard to beat petunias. Some gardeners have favorite cultivars, which they plant faithfully year after year for a beautiful display. Some prefer to try something new each season. If you get hooked on petunias, you will never be bored.

Like their cousins, flowering tobacco, tobacco, potatoes and tomatoes, the two species that are the parents of our garden petunias come from South America. In the wild, *Petunia violacea* and *P. nyctaginiflora* are perennial, and while they can be overwintered, they are so inexpensive and readily available that we grow them as annuals.

The most popular category of petunia is the **single grandiflora**. These have large single blooms in a dazzling array of shapes and colors. Some of the most popular single grandifloras are:

BICOLOR:	'Blue Frost'	blue center with white ruffled edges
	'Penny Candy'	red and white striped with ruffled edges
	'Red Picotee'	red and white, Fleuroselect winner
	'Ultra Crimson Star'	red and white, All-America Selection 1988
WHITE:	'Supermagic White'	compact and weather tolerant, non-stretching

WHITE (CONT'D)	'Ultra White'	base branching, dwarf, good for containers
	'White Cascade'	good for containers
	'White Flash'	early large pure white, rain resistant
YELLOW:	'Yellow Magic'	ruffled butter yellow, less fading than some
PURPLE AND BLUE:	'Blue Cloud'	velvety violet, compact habit
	'Royal Cascade'	deep velvety purple
	'Sky Cascade'	clear sky blue
	'Sugar Daddy'	a popular favorite; bright reddish-purple with deeper wine-red veins; great in containers
	'Supercascade Lilac'	smooth lavender with white throat
RED:	'Red Cascade'	bright red for beds or pots
	'Red Flash'	very compact and weather resistant
	'Ultra Red'	very dwarf base-branching plants
PINK:	'Appleblossom'	compact habit and weather resistant
	'Blush Supercascade'	pale pink with a rose throat

In general, all of the 'Ultra' series are very good. They come in 11 separate colors. The 'Cascade' or 'Supercascade' series are outstanding in containers because they will trail over the edge, but they can also be used in beds.

Single multiflora petunias have smaller flowers, but more of them. They are more widely used for massed bedding in the garden or in parks. Popular cultivars include:

| BICOLOR: | 'Starfire' | deep scarlet with a white star |

WHITE:	'Paleface'	white with a cream throat
YELLOW:	'Summer Sun'	the best yellow petunia to date
PURPLE:	'Sugar Plum'	reddish-purple with wine-red veins

The 'Resisto' series of single multifloras was developed in Europe to withstand cool wet summer conditions and they perform well here. They also perform well in hot, dry summers. There are six separate colors available: 'Red Star' (red and white bicolor), 'Blue Star' (blue and white bicolor), 'Blue', 'Scarlet', 'White' and 'Rose', as well as a mix.

There are **double grandiflora** and **double multiflora** petunias available that resemble carnations. They are not as weather resistant as the singles, but would do well under cover of a south-facing balcony. The 1987 AAS winner 'Purple Pirouette' has large, deep purple blooms with white edges.

Bloomtime: May to frost.

Height: 6–10 inches (15–25 cm), depending on the cultivar.

Light and soil: Full or half-day sun and any well-drained soil. Fertilize and water well in summer.

How to grow: Young plants are always available from shops in spring, or they can be grown from seed. Sow in early March and cover seeds very lightly, as light aids germination. At 70°F (21°C) soil temperature, this takes 10–12 days. Use bottom heat if possible. Set hardened-off plants out in late May, spacing them 12 inches (30 cm) apart. Pinch the growing tips often during the season to encourage bushiness. Removing old flowers keeps plants looking top-notch, but it's a chore because plants are sticky.

Pests and diseases: Petunias are generally trouble-free, but APHIDS may infest new growth on young plants. Occasionally, VIRUS diseases attack petunias, causing the plants to be stunted. Basal and root ROTS may cause plants to collapse in cold, wet soil, a good reason not to set out plants too early.

Uses: Massed in flower beds, used for edging, in containers and window boxes. In hanging baskets, petunias are best on their own.

Phlox drummondii "annual phlox" POLEMONIACEAE
(Figure 3-9)

The delicate annual phlox is related to two fine perennials, border phlox (*Phlox paniculata*) and rockery phlox (*P. subulata*). They all are native to

North America; the annual, from Texas, is half-hardy in the Pacific coast region. The stems are somewhat trailing and each ends in a cluster of 5-petalled flowers. Leaves are bright green. Flower colors include soft shades of white, red, pink, maroon and lavender. Phlox have an old-fashioned look and are easy to grow.

The cultivar 'Twinkle' has star-shaped blooms and is only 6 inches (15 cm) high. It is delightful in a window box. 'Cecily' grows to 8 inches (20 cm) high and many flowers have a contrasting eye. 'Petticoat Mixed' is generally available as young plants in shops in spring; it has good sun and drought tolerance. There are also taller types suitable for cutting that are not generally sold in shops.

Bloomtime: July to September.

Height: 6–14 inches (15–36 cm), depending on the cultivar.

Light and soil: Prefers full sun and a moist soil to which some organic matter has been added. Water well in dry weather.

How to grow: Young plants are generally available from shops in spring; if possible, buy plants that are "green," that is, not in bloom yet. Phlox can easily be started from seed. Sow indoors in March, ⅓ inch (.3 cm) deep, directly into individual pots (they do not like to be transplanted). Seeds need 60°F (15°C) soil temperature and total darkness to germinate. When the seedlings are up, grow them on at 55°F (13°C). Plant out in late May, spacing them 9 inches (23 cm) apart. Or sow directly in the garden in April for late June bloom. The weakest seedlings often have the brightest colors, so bear this in mind when thinning. Removing old flowers extends the flowering period.

Pests and diseases: SLUGS like young plants.

Uses: Beds, borders, window boxes and planters.

"Pocketbook flower" see *Calceolaria*
"Polka dot plant" see *Hypoestes*
"Polyanthus" see *Primula*
"Poor-man's orchid" see *Schizanthus*
"Poppy, Iceland" see *Papaver nudicaule*
"Poppy, Shirley" see *Papaver rhoeas*

Portulaca grandiflora "moss rose" "portulaca" PORTULACACEAE
(Figure 4-7)

Portulaca is an annual sun lover from Brazil and Argentina with 1-inch (2.5-cm) rose-like single or double flowers. Colors include white, pink, rose, red and yellow in shades that look festive planted as a mixed group.

The trailing stems bear ½-inch (1.3-cm), sausage-shaped, fleshy leaves. While most portulacas close their blooms on a cloudy day, two cultivars, 'Afternoon Delight' and 'Cloudbeater Mixed', stay open all day.

Bloomtime: June to September, or until heavy fall rains damage the flowers.

Height: To 6 inches (15 cm) high by 12 inches (30 cm) across for most cultivars.

Light and soil: A hot, sunny spot with very well-drained (even dry) sandy soil.

How to grow: Young plants are generally available from shops in spring, or they can easily be grown from seed. Sow seeds indoors in March, directly into small pots to avoid transplanting. Press seeds into soil but do not cover, as light is required for germination. Germination, at 70°F (21°C) soil temperature, takes about 10 days. Grow on at 60–65°F (15–18°C) with lots of light and not too much water. Plant out at the end of May, spacing 6 inches (15 cm) apart.

Pests and diseases: If planted out too early, plants can DAMP OFF. APHIDS can occasionally be a problem.

Uses: Edging for paths and at the front of sunny borders, trailing over the top of a wall or planted in a rock garden.

"Pouch flower" see *Calceolaria*

Primula xpolyantha "polyanthus" "primrose" "primula" PRIMULACEAE (Figure 7-9)

Polyanthus are hybrids of three species: *Primula vulgaris* (also called *P. acaulis*), English primrose; *P. veris*, cowslip; and a third species over which there is some disagreement. At any rate, all parents are native to Europe and polyanthus have been in gardens for as long as there have been gardens in Europe. *P. veris* was thought to have many curative properties. There is an old French saying, "Qui a du bugle et du sanicle fait au chirurgien le nicle." (Who possesses ajuga and primulas has no need of a doctor.) In 1768, a small book devoted to the primulas indicated them for curing blemishes, headaches, weeping, gallstones, red eyes, fever, coughing and wounds.

In the Pacific coast region, we plant polyanthus to cheer us up during our long rainy springs. They are sold in bloom in shops in fall and very early spring and can be used as winter bedding. In following years, blooms usually appear in spring only. The dazzling array of colors includes white, yellow, orange, peach, pink, rose, red, lavender, purple and maroon, often with a contrasting eye or edge to the petals. The five-petalled flowers cluster above the rosette of bright green basal leaves. In a group of seedlings, some plants will be fragrant.

Bloomtime: Early spring.

Height: 6–10 inches (15–25 cm) , depending on the cultivar.

Light and soil: Full sun or shade and a moist but well-drained soil to which some organic matter has been added. They do not like to dry out.

How to grow: Young plants are generally available from shops in spring, which is the easiest way to get them. Because the seeds need cool temperatures to germinate, they are germinated commercially in bulb companies' coolers that are empty in the summer. Seedlings are shipped to growers in August for potting on and sale in bloom in the fall. Home growers can germinate the seeds in a sunny window sill in February for bloom the following spring; air temperature of about 70°F (21°C) is perfect. Seeds take up to 4 weeks to germinate; fresh seeds germinate best. Press seeds gently into the potting mix, but do not cover with mix. Keep moist. Set young plants out in May. Mature plants can also be propagated by division in July; dig up the whole plant and gently pull apart the separate clumps.

Pests and diseases: Polyanthus are popular with ROOT WEEVILS, SLUGS, SNAILS, and CUTWORMS. There are a number of viruses and fungi that may attack polyanthus, but they are generally healthy in the garden.

Uses: As winter and early spring bedding, polyanthus are perfect for an informal or woodland setting, at the front of a mixed border, as an edging, or in containers. Try them in a large pot by the front door with winter pansies and some spring bulbs.

"Prince's feather" see *Amaranthus*

Psylliostachys suworowii see *Limonium*

"Quaking grass" see *Avena*

Rudbeckia hirta "black-eyed susan" "gloriosa daisy" ASTERACEAE
(Figure 7-10)

Although black-eyed susans are short-lived perennials, they bloom the first year from seed and make colorful bedding plants and cut flowers. Native to eastern North America, daisy-like blooms up to 3 inches (7.5 cm) across have brown centers and petals in shades of orange. The leaves are long and hairy, and taper to a point. 'Marmalade' grows to 22 inches (56 cm) and has bright gold petals; 'Rustic Dwarf Mixed' is the same height but its blooms are yellow, orange, gold, bronze or mahogany, with contrasting rings of color. Both are excellent. 'Goldilocks' won a Fleuroselect medal for its compact height of 10 inches (25 cm), double blooms that look like golden petticoats and the fact that the masses of new flowers hide the old flowers. For something different, 'Irish Eyes' has 4½-inch (11-cm) flowers with gold petals and green centers on 30-inch (76-cm) plants.

Bloomtime: August to October.

Height: 1–3 feet (.9–1.2 m), depending on the cultivar.

Light and soil: Prefers full sun and any well-drained soil to which some organic matter has been added.

How to grow: Young plants are not usually available with the bedding plants, but try looking for them with the perennials. They are easily grown from seed sown in March. Germination, at 70°F (21°C) soil temperature, takes about 20 days. Set young plants out from April on, spacing them 12–18 inches (30–46 cm) apart, depending on the cultivar.

Pests and diseases: Watch for SLUGS and SNAILS.

Uses: Bedding and cut flowers, in borders and in large containers.

"Sage, mealy-cup" see *Salvia farinacea*
"Sage, scarlet" see *Salvia splendens*

Salpiglossis sinuata "salpiglossis" "painted-tongue" SOLANACEAE
(Figure 5-10)

Salpiglossis is a delightful change for gardeners who find that some annuals are too bright and hard to work into a garden scheme. In the same family as the petunia, salpiglossis also produces trumpet-shaped flowers all summer and has sticky stems. There the similarity ends. Salpiglossis is an elegant upright plant with wiry stems. Blooms are in shades of yellow, purple and red, with delicate veining and markings in contrasting colors, reminiscent of a stained glass window. This native of Chile should be grown as a half-hardy annual and does best in a warm summer.

'Splash' blooms profusely, and 'Bolero' has huge blooms veined in gold; both reach 24 inches (61 cm). 'Dwarf Friendship Mixed' is early-blooming and compact. 'Diablo' is also to be recommended.

Bloomtime: July to frost.

Height: 15–24 inches (38–61 cm), depending on the cultivar.

Light and soil: Prefers full sun and a rich well-drained soil. Add some organic matter if possible. On poorer soil 'Splash' does better than other cultivars.

How to grow: Although young plants are not generally available from shops, they can be grown from seed. Sow indoors in March, gently pressing seeds into the soil, but do not cover. Complete darkness is required for germination, which, at 70°F (21°C) soil temperature, takes about 20 days. Set young plants out in late May, spacing them 12 inches (30 cm) apart. Tall types can be staked with small twigs. Remove old flowers to encourage more bloom.

Pests and diseases: APHIDS may infest new growth and root ROT may cause plants to collapse in a very wet summer. Delay planting until June if weather is very cold.

Uses: Mid-height planting in a mixed border. Salpiglossis is useful for filling in between new shrub plantings as it has an upright habit. Try several plants in a large planter with shorter annuals such as purple alyssum, 'Cambridge Blue' lobelia or dimorphotheca. They make excellent cut flowers if you don't mind the sticky stems.

Salvia farinacea "blue salvia" "mealy-cup sage" LAMIACEAE
(Figures 5-11 and 7-7)

For many years seen mainly in park plantings, this lovely, half-hardy perennial is now showing up in many garden centers. Originally from New Mexico and Texas, blue salvia makes a great addition to a bedding scheme or mixed border. It is an elegant plant, with small, blue, pea-like flowers on tall spikes above gray-green foliage. Blue is always a welcome color in any garden, and this plant also offers an attractive bushy habit. The most widely grown cultivar is 'Victoria', which is a Fleuroselect winner.

Bloomtime: June or July to October. Plants look fresh right up to the frost.
Height: 18 inches (46 cm).
Light and soil: Prefers full sun and any well-drained soil.
How to grow: Young plants are becoming more widely available from shops in spring, or they can be started from seed. Sow in small individual pots inMarch. Do not cover, as light is required for germination. At 70°F (21°C) soil temperature, germination takes about 14 days. Set young plants out in late May, spacing them 12 inches (30 cm) apart.
Pests and diseases: Generally trouble-free.
Uses: Pattern plantings, edging and bedding. Excellent in containers and window boxes. Long lasting cut or dried flower.

Salvia splendens "red salvia" "scarlet sage" LAMIACEAE
(Figure 4-8)

One of the most widely planted of summer bedding plants, red salvia must be used with care in the home garden due to its vibrant red color–if over-used it certainly does not create a restful atmosphere. The bright green leaves are rounded at the base and taper to a long point, with teeth along the edges. The individual red flowers, each surrounded by a red bract that makes them appear even larger, form a tall spike.

In its native Brazil, *Salvia splendens* is a subshrub, but it will not survive our winters. It blooms quickly from seed and is grown here as a half-hardy annual. Purple and white cultivars of this species of salvia have also been developed, but the white flowers often fade to brown and are untidy looking.

Bloomtime: Dwarf cultivars begin to bloom in late May or June; taller ones begin in August. Both continue to the frost.

Height: 10–30 inches (25–76 cm), depending on the cultivar.

Light and soil: Full sun or very light shade and fertile, well-drained soil.

How to grow: Young plants are readily available from shops in spring, or they can be started from seed. Sow seeds indoors in March, but do not cover, as light is required for germination, which, at 70°F (21°C) soil temperature, takes about 14 days. Grow on at 60°F (15°C) soil temperature. Feed lightly when transplanted with one of the liquid fertilizers (see page 18). Do not overfertilize seedlings or they will burn. Set young plants out in late May, spacing them 12 inches (30 cm) apart, closer for dwarf cultivars.

Pests and diseases: Generally trouble-free.

Uses: Pattern plantings, edging or borders. Best with white, yellow or blue flowers or silver dusty miller.

Sanvitalia procumbens "creeping zinnia" ASTERACEAE
(Figures 6-3 and 6-8)

Creeping zinnia is covered with ½-inch (1-cm) flowers with yellow petals and black disks, resembling tiny sunflowers. The leaves are simple, tapering to a gentle point. As the name suggests, the habit is creeping, which makes this Mexican native a good addition to a sunny planter or hanging basket. The cultivar 'Flore Pleno' has double flowers, giving it an extra row of petals, but the attractive black center still shows. 'Mandarin Orange' is the first orange-flowered creeping zinnia and an AAS winner.

Bloomtime: June if started indoors, July if started outdoors. Continues blooming well right to the frost, even in rainy weather.

Height: 6 inches (15 cm), spreading to a foot (30 cm) or so across.

Light and soil: Prefers full sun or partial shade and any well-drained soil to which some organic matter has been added. It tolerates heat and drought.

How to grow: Although young plants are not generally available from shops, they are easily grown from seed. Sow in March indoors for earlier bloom. Germination, at 60°F (15°C) soil temperature, takes about 10 days. Set hardened-off plants out in late May, spacing them 3 inches (7.5 cm) apart, or sow directly in the garden in May.

Pests and diseases: Generally trouble-free.

Uses: Trailing over the edge of containers or retaining walls, in hanging baskets, either alone or with other bedding plants.

"Satin flower" see *Clarkia*

***Schizanthus* hybrids** "schizanthus" "butterfly flower" "poor-man's orchid"
SOLANACEAE
(Figure 4-9)

Schizanthus is a lovely annual which is very popular with those who know it. Many gardeners first see it in the mixed hanging baskets that are sold for Mother's Day. It trails and is covered with dozens of small, orchid-like flowers in shades of pink, rose, red, white, yellow or mauve, attractively marked and spotted. The foliage is bright green and finely cut, almost fern-like. As seedlings are rarely in bloom in packs in garden centers in spring and may not be labelled, it is not always easy to spot. You may need to ask shop staff to point it out.

In its native Chile, the butterfly flower grows on the cool slopes of the Andes, and here on the Pacific coast it also prefers cool weather. In a very hot summer, it tends to stop blooming, but provides a marvelous show in June and July. For this reason, it is best grown in containers rather than right in the garden, where it will leave a gap if it fades out.

Bloomtime: June to August or September, depending on the season. Make a second sowing to extend the season of bloom.

Height: 10–24 inches (25–61 cm) in height or trailing, depending on the cultivar.

Light and soil: Full sun or light shade and rich, moist soil with added organic matter.

How to grow: Young plants are generally available from shops in spring, but they seem to sell out fast. They can also be started from seed sown in late March. Press seeds into soil but do not cover. Set pots or flats in total darkness. Germination, at 60°F (15°C) soil temperature, takes about 15 days. Do not set out young plants until late May. Seedlings can be started again in May for autumn bloom.

Pests and diseases: APHIDS may infest new growths. Overwatering may result in root ROT.

Uses: Lovely in hanging baskets and trailing over the edge of containers,

Schizanthus can also be used right in the garden, planted near bedding plants, such as browallia and China asters, which are at their best late in the summer.

"Sea lavender" see *Limonium*

Senecio cineraria (*Cineraria maritima, Centaurea maritima*) "dusty miller" ***Chrysanthemum ptarmiciflorum*** (*Pyrethrum ptarmiciflorum*) "silver lace dusty miller" ASTERACEAE
(Figure 6-10)
Although they are in different genera, dusty miller and silver lace dusty miller are grouped together here because of their similar appearance, uses and cultivation. There is much confusion over their botanical names. Dusty miller is sold in seed catalogues as *Centaurea* and *Cineraria*. Silver lace dusty miller is never listed under its botanical name, but is thrown in with the other dusty millers or sometimes called *Pyrethrum*. In this case, it's probably best to look for the plants by common name and read the description carefully, as there are other plants which are less often called dusty miller.

Dusty miller is a member of one of the largest genera of flowering plants. There are 2,000–3,000 species of *Senecio* in all parts of the world. It is an evergreen subshrub in its Mediterranean home, and usually survives our mild coastal winters. It is grown for its decorative foliage, rather than its yellow daisy-like blooms. The leaves are covered with a matting of fine, white hair which gives them a silvery appearance. There are three excellent cultivars on the market. 'Diamond' is the most finely cut, with indentations right into the midrib of the leaf. 'Silverdust' somewhat resembles an oak leaf, with indentations about halfway into the leaf. 'Cirrus' has leaves with scallops around the edges, rather than indentations. They all grow to 12–18 inches (30–46 cm) in the garden. Park seed catalogue lists 'Silver Queen', which grows to only 8 inches (20 cm).

Silverlace dusty miller has aromatic foliage and seldom gets enough heat in our climate to produce its white daisy-like blooms. It also seems a bit slower to get going in a cool spring and has a more upright growth habit than dusty miller. Pinch the growing tips often when young to encourage bushiness. The leaves are more finely cut than the most finely cut dusty miller, hence the common name. It will reach 24 inches (61 cm) in a warm summer.
Bloomtime: Neither of these two plants are grown for their blooms. Dusty miller will bloom late summer some years, or the following spring if over-

wintered, but it is best to pinch off the long flower stalks to keep the plants compact. Silverlace dusty miller seldom blooms outdoors in the Pacific coast region.

Height: 8–24 inches (20–61 cm), depending on the cultivar.

Light and soil: Prefers full sun and any well-drained soil. Both types of dusty miller will tolerate poor dry soil.

How to grow: Young plants are readily available from shops in spring, or they can be started from seed. Sow seeds indoors in early March and cover only lightly, as light aids germination. At 70°F (21°C) soil temperature, this takes about 14 days. Maintain humidity and even soil temperature. Set hardened-off plants out in late May, spacing them 12 inches (30 cm) apart. Pinch growing tips to encourage branching. If flower shoots develop in late summer, it is best to cut them off. If desired, leave plants of dusty miller in the ground in the fall, where they will look attractive through most winters. They can be left in for another season, but will be more compact with heavy pinching. Because they are usually winter hardy, dusty miller are also sold in shops in fall for winter bedding. Their silver leaves are an excellent foil to winter pansies, ornamental kale and primulas.

Pests and diseases: Generally trouble-free.

Uses: Dusty miller looks neat separating various low bedding plants in formal pattern plantings. Use it as an edging for flower beds or rose gardens. Silverlace dusty miller is less dense, so it gives a less formal effect. Use it in a mixed border. It also cuts well, adding softness to bouquets.

Setcreasea pallida '**Purple Heart**', *Tradescantia albiflora, T. fluminensis,* and *Zebrina pendula* "wandering Jew" COMMELINACEAE

Although they are in different genera, these four species are grouped together here because of their similar appearance, uses and cultivation. Like ivy, nepeta and silver nettle vine, they are grown for the contribution their foliage makes to a mixed container planting. They are often sold as houseplants and are easily recognized by the fact that the base of their leaves wrap around the creeping stems. All are native to Texas, Mexico or South America, where they are perennial, but they do not survive frost.

Setcreasea pallida 'Purple Heart' has deep purple leaves up to 6 inches (15 cm), which are covered with soft hair. It produces small violet flowers with three petals.

The two species of *Tradescantia* have shimmering leaves to 3 inches (7.5 cm) long produced along zig-zag stems. Leaves may be green or striped with white, purple or yellow, depending on the cultivar. The small three-petalled flowers are white. The species of this genus hybridize easily, and there are many hybrids available.

Zebrina pendula is similar to *Tradescantia albiflora*, except that it has rose-purple flowers.

Bloomtime: Although grown for foliage rather than bloom, wandering Jew produces small flowers during summer (or winter if grown as a houseplant).

Height: Trails to 18 inches (46 cm).

Light and soil: Part shade or shade and rich, moist soil.

How to grow: Young plants are generally available from shops in spring. They may be with the bedding plants or with houseplants. They are easily propagated from cuttings taken at any time of year. Because they do not tolerate frost, do not set plants out until the danger of frost is past, in late May.

Pests and diseases: Leaves may be eaten by SLUGS. A PHYSIOLOGICAL DISORDER causes leaves to turn brown and fall off; this is not a disease.

Uses: Trailing from planters and hanging baskets, with other bedding plants.

"Silver lace dusty miller" see *Senecio*
"Silver nettle vine" see *Lamiastrum*
"Slipper flower" see *Calceolaria*
"Snapdragon" see *Antirrhinum*
"Spider flower" see *Cleome*
"Star-of-Bethlehem" see *Campanula isophylla*
"Star-of-the-veldt" see *Dimorphotheca*
"Statice, common, Russian and rat-tail" see *Limonium*
"Stock, common" see *Matthiola incana*
"Stock, evening or night scented" see *Matthiola longipetala*
"Strawflower" see *Helichrysum*
"Summer cypress" see *Kochia*
"Sunflower" see *Helianthus*
"Sweet pea" see *Lathyrus*
"Sweet william" see *Dianthus barbatus*

Tagetes erecta "African marigold"
Tagetes filifolia "Irish lace"
Tagetes patula "French marigold"
Tagetes tenuifolia (*T. signata pumila*) "signet marigold" ASTERACEAE
(Figures 7-7, 7-11, 7-12 and 8-6)

In areas with hot summers, marigolds may not continue blooming all summer, but here near the Pacific ocean, they bloom right up to the frost if well watered, often looking brighter in the warm days of September and October. There are hundreds of cultivars of marigold on the market, derived from four species of half-hardy annuals native to Mexico. Despite the fact that marigolds originally came from Mexico, they tolerate wet weather quite well, especially the French marigolds. (I have not seen an explanation of why the terms "French" and "African" are used when they are all from Mexico). Marigolds have a distinctly pungent aroma.

African marigolds. Forming the tallest group, the parent species of these cultivars reaches 3 feet (91 cm), with blooms up to 8 inches (20 cm) across in the wild. Leaves are divided into many long, dark green leaflets. A number of seed series with large double blooms like huge pompons have been developed from this species. The 'Inca' series is highly recommended for 3½-inch (9-cm) blooms on 12-inch (30-cm) plants. Colors include orange, yellow or gold. They are not bothered by rainy or hot weather and bloom right up to the frost.

The 'Galore' series has won AAS and Fleuroselect awards. Blooms are sponge-like, to 4 inches (10 cm) across, and old blooms disappear under new ones, so little deadheading is required. 'Moonshot' is another semi-dwarf African marigold which is still popular, reaching 14 inches (36 cm).

'Toreador', an AAS winner, grows to 30 inches (76 cm) and has rich orange blooms. The tall cultivars 'Doubloon'(yellow) and 'Double Eagle' (orange) are often available in 4-inch (10-cm) pots in shops in the spring.

The African marigolds are daylength-sensitive. For this reason, it is best to sow seeds during the middle of March. If sown later, seedlings must be restricted to only 8 hours of light each day for two weeks during the seedling stage. This means covering the flats with black plastic or moving the flats into a dark closet after 8 hours. Otherwise, blooming will begin later and last for a shorter period. Cover seeds with ¼ inch (.6 cm) of potting mix. Germination, at 70°F (21°C) soil temperature, takes about 7 days. Set hardened-off plants out in late May, spaced 12 inches (30 cm) apart.

French marigolds. *Tagetes patula* is the parent of the French marigolds. It grows only 6–18 inches (15–46 cm) tall in the wild and has smaller flower than *T. erecta*. Leaflets are small, giving a more delicate effect than the foliage of the African marigolds. Cultivars with single flowers have one row of petals around the central disk. They are appealing for their freshness and simplicity. The 'Belle' series is triploid and consequently does not set seed. In terms of plant performance, that translates into nonstop bloom in all kinds of weather. Although a lower percentage of seeds germinates, plants bloom approximately 40 days after sowing, a good 2–3 weeks earlier than similar cultivars which are not triploid. For yellow blooms, try 'Susie Wong', which is sometimes available in shops. 'Little Nell' is gold with a red stain at the base of each petal.

Most dwarf French marigolds do not have single flowers. They fall into two categories. The crested types have a pouf of petals at the center (the crest), set off by one or more rows of petals around the edge. The broad-petalled types have larger petals, evenly spaced over the flower. Outstanding crested types include the 'Boy' series, which is available in orange, yellow, gold, yellow/maroon bicolor, orange/mahogany bicolor and a mixture of all six. Plants reach 8–10 inches (20–25 cm) in height. The 'Sophia' series is excellent in the broad-petalled class. Separate colors include 'Scarlet Sophia', 'Queen Sophia' (red with a gold margin on each petal), as well as yellow, orange and mixed seed strains. Plants grow to 10–12 inches (25–30 cm). Both the 'Boy' and 'Sophia' series are available in most seed catalogues and some of the colors are usually available in shops as young plants. Another excellent, widely grown, dwarf French marigold is 'Lemon Drop', which reaches 8 inches (20 cm) and is covered with small yellow pompons.

French marigolds are not daylength-sensitive so they are very easy to grow from seed at home. Sow seeds and cover with ¼ inch (.6 cm) potting soil in mid-March. Germination, at 60–70F (15–21°C), takes 7 days. Set hardened-off plants out in late May, spacing them 8–12 inches (20–30 cm) apart, depending on the cultivar.

Afro-French marigolds. A new class of marigolds combining the dwarfness of the French with the doubleness of bloom of the Africans was created by crossing both. They are called Afro-French marigolds and reach 12–16 inches (30–41 cm) in height. The offspring are triploid and therefore, like the 'Belle' series, the rate of germination is low. Because the flowers cannot set seed, plants put all their vigor into blooming, becoming very free-flowering. Stokes sell seed for 'Saffron' (yellow), 'Ginger' (gold) and 'Spice' (orange), all of which are recommended. Sow seeds in late March, just covering with ¼ inch (.6 cm) of vermiculite. Germination, at 70°F (21°C) soil temperature, takes about 14 days. Restrict light to nine hours each day for two weeks after seedlings are up. When transplanting into larger pots, watch for "mule" seedlings; they are unusually large and should be removed. Grow on at 55–60°F (10–15°C). Young plants can start out with single or reddish blooms due to low light and cool temperatures, but will become double when the weather warms. Set hardened-off plants out in late May, spacing them 12 inches (30 cm) apart.

Specialty cultivars. *Tagetes tenuifolia* is the parent of several very dwarf marigolds with dime-sized single or tufted blooms, fine ferny foliage and a mounding habit of growth. They are sometimes referred to as signet marigolds, rock garden marigolds or as tagetes. The outer petals have distinct notches. Cultivars include 'Golden Gem' and 'Lemon Gem', which grow to 6 inches (15 cm) and 9 inches (23 cm) respectively. 'Tangerine Gem' reaches 12 inches (30 cm) and is interesting in small flower arrangements. Stokes and Thompson and Morgan both sell the seed. Follow seeding directions for French marigolds. Set hardened-off plants out in late May, spacing them 8 inches (20 cm) apart.

Tagetes filifolia, Irish lace, is grown for its ferny foliage rather than its tiny white flowers, which appear late in the summer. It makes a bright green mound of edging in bedding-out schemes.

There are many cultivars offered by seed companies and they are always trying new ones. Don't be afraid to try something different. In fact, from time to time Thompson and Morgan offer a collection of new cultivars, which are not yet on the market, for home gardeners to grow and evaluate.

Bloomtime: May or June to frost.

Height: 6–30 inches (15–76 cm), depending on the cultivar.

Light and soil: Prefer full sun and a moderately rich, well-drained soil. They will tolerate poor, dry soils.

How to grow: Young plants are readily available from shops in spring, or they can be started from seed. See specific instructions for each type of marigold above.

Pests and diseases: If planted too early, they may collapse due to foot ROT. SLUGS also eat the leaves of marigolds.

Uses: African marigolds are suitable for the middle of the flower border and the taller types are good cut flowers. French marigolds and Afro-French are useful for edging and lovely in containers. Signet marigolds are attractive in rock gardens and containers. Irish lace is an unusual edging plant, suitable also for pattern plantings, as are the dwarf French marigolds.

"Tasselflower" see *Amaranthus*

Thunbergia alata "black-eyed-susan vine" ACANTHACEAE
(Figure 6-11)

A perennial vine in tropical Africa, black-eyed-susan vine is grown as an annual in the Pacific coast region. It has 3-inch (7.5-cm), arrow-head-shaped leaves along stems that twine counter-clockwise. The flowers have five petals that open up from a narrow, dark purple tube. This gives the effect of a dark hole at the center of the flower and is quite striking. Flowers are most often orange, but mixed seed with cream and yellow flowers is available. With some protection, such as a cool greenhouse or sun porch, it may overwinter.

Bloomtime: May to frost.

Height: Climbs to at least 3 feet (1.2 m). If well-fertilized, many shoots develop from the base, making a dense tangle of growth.

Light and soil: Full sun or part shade, and a well-drained soil. In the garden, plants do not seem to mind a bit of bark mulch around their roots to keep them cool and moist.

How to grow: Young plants are sometimes available from shops in spring, or they can be started from seed. Sow and cover lightly. Germination, at 60–70°F (15–21°C) soil temperature, takes about 14 days. Grow seedlings on at 60°F (15°C). Set hardened-off plants out in late May, spacing them 12 inches (30 cm) apart in the garden.

Pests and diseases: Generally trouble-free.

Uses: Black-eyed-susan vine can be grown up a trellis or into a shrub in the garden. Grow also in hanging baskets, either alone or with other plants. It tends to climb up the wires of the basket rather than trail down.

"Tickseed" see *Coreopsis*

Torenia fournieri "wishbone flower" SCROPHULARIACEAE
(Figure 2-11)

Wishbone flower is so named because the small stamens resemble a wishbone. The flowers look like small snapdragons, to which the plants are related. They are a rich, velvety violet with lighter blue and yellow markings. They are produced in abundance in June and continue over a long period if kept cool, shaded and moist. The pale green leaves are narrow, pointed and toothed. A half-hardy annual, *Torenia* is native to Vietnam.

Bloomtime: June onwards, depending on the season.

Height: Up to 12 inches (30 cm).

Light and soil: Part shade and rich moist soil.

How to grow: Although young plants are not generally available from shops, they can be grown from seed. Sow seeds indoors in March but do not cover, as light is required for germination. Germination, at 70°F (21°C) soil temperature, takes about 14 days. Set hardened-off plants out in late

May, spacing them 8 inches (20 cm) apart. Support lightly with twiggy branches.

Pests and diseases: Generally trouble-free.

Uses: Try it as an unusual addition to a shady container or bed.

Tradescantia see *Setcreasea*
"Tuberous begonia" see *Begonia*

Tropaeolum majus "nasturtium" TROPAEOLACEAE
(Figures 1-11, 6-3 and 8-6)

When first introduced to Europe from Peru in the 1600s, this popular plant was known as Indian cress, because the Peruvian Indians used the pungent leaves in food. Hence, the original botanical name was *Nasturtium indicum*. (Watercress is *Nasturtium officinale*.) Later, Linnaeus, the Swedish botanist who reorganized botanical nomenclature, changed the name to *Tropaeolum majus*. The generic name refers to the Greek word *tropaion* meaning trophy. In ancient Greece, this was a tree on which victors hung the shields and helmets of those they had conquered in battle. Linnaeus must have seen in the round leaves and pointed flowers the shields and helmets of perished Greek warriors.

Although perennial in the highlands of Mexico and South America, nasturtiums do not like even a hint of frost. All parts of nasturtium have a peppery taste due to an oil they contain; flower buds and young leaves are used in salads and the fresh green seeds can be pickled in the same manner as capers. Of course, do not eat plant parts if any harmful pesticides have been used. The petioles (stalks which attach the leaves to the stems) are able to coil, thus allowing the plants to climb.

The most widely available cultivar in shops in spring is the 'Jewel Mixed', which includes semi-double flowers of cream, orange, yellow, red, pink and bicolors. The 'Whirlibird' series features flowers which sit facing up on the vine and are more visible. Separate colors include gold, scarlet, tangerine, mahogany, tangerine, orange, and cherry. 'Alaska Mixed', a Stokes introduction, has very attractive variegated foliage and is an excellent addition to hanging baskets and other containers (shown in Figure 6-3).'Empress of India' is a cultivar of the species *Tropaeolum minus*, which is similar to the common nasturtium, but is smaller.

Bloomtime: June to September.

Height: 12 inches (30 cm), or more trailing or climbing.

Light and soil: Prefers full sun, but tolerates light shade. Any well-drained, preferably sandy (even dry) soil. Do not use a fertilizer high in nitrogen or the plant will produce huge, deep green leaves and no bloom.

How to grow: Young plants are generally available from shops in spring, or they can be started from seed. Seeds can be sown directly in the garden, especially in a warm, dry spring. If the weather is very cool and wet, it is best to sow indoors in individual 3-inch (7.5-cm) pots so seeds will not rot. Germination, at 60–70°F (15–21°C) soil temperature, takes about 14 days. Seedlings grow quickly; they can be seeded in April and set out in late May, 8–12 inches (20–30 cm) apart, depending on the cultivar.

Pests and diseases: APHIDS are a serious problem with nasturtiums; they appear so predictably and in such great numbers that it is impossible to ignore them. Insecticidal soap will burn nasturtium foliage and should not be used. Organic gardeners use nasturtiums as companion plants near crops which are susceptible to aphid infestations hoping all the aphids will be attracted to the nasturtiums instead.

Uses: Train up trellises; allow to trail from containers and hanging baskets. They can also be grown in the garden as ground cover, trailing over walls or scrambling into deciduous shrubs. Because seeds are large and germinate readily, children enjoy starting nasturtiums.

Verbena x*hybrida* "garden verbena"
Verbena peruviana "Peruvian verbena"
Verbena rigida (*V. venosa*) "vervain"
Verbena canadensis (*V. aubletia*) "trailing verbena" VERBENACEAE
(Figures 4-10 and 8-11)

Garden verbena is an easily obtainable summer bedding plant. The flowers are very bright and fresh, but it is not as free-blooming as some bedding plants and is very susceptible to mildew. Gray-green leaves are triangular in outline with regularly spaced teeth along the leaf margin. Stems and leaves are covered with fine hairs. Flowers appear in a cluster at the end of stalks: each has 5 petals opening from a 1-inch (2.5-cm) tube. Colors typically include scarlet, white and purple, often with a white eye. The habit of some cultivars is somewhat floppy and open. These hybrids are derived mainly from *V. peruviana* and other species from South America, which are all perennials there. 'Trinidad' is an AAS winner with rose blooms and a compact upright habit.

Peruvian verbena has brilliant red flowers with a white eye. It also has a trailing habit and is a welcome addition to a rock garden or hanging basket. It will sometimes survive a winter if given some protection.

Vervain is an upright grower with long, narrow, toothed leaves and lilac or white flowers. It is attractive planted with zonal geraniums.

139

Trailing verbena has stems which have about 2 inches (5 cm) between each set of leaves. This open rambling habit make it perfect for growing from containers and hanging baskets. The leaves are darker green than those of the garden verbena, and the indentations into the leaves are deeper and less regular. Flowers also cluster at the end of long flower stalks. Colors include vivid purple, red, pink and white.

Bloomtime: June to frost.

Height: 6–18 inches (15–46 cm), depending on the cultivar.

Light and soil: Prefers full sun and any well-drained soil to which some organic matter has been added.

How to grow: Young plants are generally available from shops in spring, the easiest way to acquire them, as seeds are tricky to germinate. If you are interested in trying it, first chill seeds in the refrigerator for 7 days in March. Sow seeds, cover with ⅛ inch (.3 cm) soil and place flats or pots in the dark. Soil temperature should be 70°F (21°C) in the day and 60°F (15°C) at night. Avoid excessive moisture. Germination is erratic and takes up to three weeks. A good germination rate is 50 to 65 percent. Set hardened-off plants out in late May, spacing them 8 inches (20 cm) apart. Pinch the growing tip to encourage bushiness. If they stop blooming, cut them back by one-third.

Pests and diseases: Verbenas are very prone to POWDERY MILDEW, especially the garden verbena. SLUGS like verbena.

Uses: Garden verbena and vervain as bedding plants; trailing verbena is outstanding for sunny containers and hanging baskets and as a ground cover; *V. peruviana* gives a nice splash of color in a rock garden.

"Vervain" see *Verbena*

Viola cornuta "viola" "tufted pansy"
Viola tricolor "johnny-jump-up"
Viola xwittrockiana (*V. hortensis*) "pansy" VIOLACEAE
(Figure 3-10)

Pansies are some of the most heart-warming flowers to grace our gardens in spring and fall. Their velvety overlapping petals in a rich tapestry of colors and their happy "faces" make the decision of which ones to buy a pleasurable dilemma. Pansies thrive in cool weather and for that reason they appear in shops in both spring and fall. Those sold in the spring are cultivars that are more heat-tolerant; those sold in fall as "winter pansies" are very cold-tolerant.

Viola cornuta, a native of Spain, is the parent of many cultivars of violas. It resembles the well-known pansy, but the flowers are smaller, 1–1½ inches (2.5–4 cm), and without "faces," and it continues blooming for a longer period in the summer. Seed can be purchased for separate colors including wine-red, blue, apricot, yellow, dark blue, white and a mixture. The 'Crystal Bowl' series are hybrids of *Viola cornuta* developed in Japan, with flowers up to 2½ inches (6 cm) across and clear bright colors. Violas reach about 8 inches (20 cm) in height.

Johnny-jump-ups have very small flowers, ¾ inch (2 cm) across, which have three colors: purple, yellow and white, hence the specific name *tricolor.* They grow to 6 inches (15 cm) high, with spreading stems and are excellent for planting with tulips and daffodils for a spring show. They are native to Europe. The common name refers to the fact that the self-sown seedlings "jump up" everywhere.

Pansies have been developed from three species, *Viola tricolor, V. lutea* and *V. altaica.* Although johnny-jump-ups have been well known and commonly grown in European gardens since about 1625, little was done in the way of hybridizing until the early 1800s, when selections were done by a pansy enthusiast in England. By the middle of that century, the British, French and Germans began developing different strains in earnest. Today there are pansies in almost every color imaginable. Some types have rich colors, some have bright colors, many have faces and some do not. Recently, the 'Imperial' series introduced delicate pastel shades; the flowers are very pretty but the plants do not bloom as much as those of the 'Universal' series, which are planted in the thousands in city parks. The 'Universal' series includes 12 different color shades and a mix. They bloom very early and plants remain compact even in some summer heat. They can be used for winter or spring pansies.

Bloomtime: Violas: June and July. Johnny-jump-ups: May to September. Pansies from a spring planting: March to July, depending on the cultivar and the season. Pansies from a fall planting: September until frost, then during mild spells in winter and again in early spring. Keeping plants well watered and removing old flowers helps extend the flowering period.

Height: 6–12 inches (15–30 cm), depending on the cultivar.

Light and soil: Sun or part shade and a moist but well-drained soil to which some organic matter has been added.

How to grow: Young plants of pansies and johnny-jump-ups are generally available from shops from late February on, but violas are not as common. In addition to being sold in small pots or packs, fall pansies are also field grown. They are grown outdoors in open ground (rather than in a green-house), dug and placed in cardboard baskets similar to those in which strawberries are sold. If you have a choice, field-grown pansies are usually the best plants to buy. Nothing can compare with growing in sun and real soil for producing compact healthy pansies.

Pansies can be grown from seed. The easiest way is to sow seeds in June in a nursery bed. An ideal spot is a row in the vegetable garden after the peas, for example, have come out. Let them grow there until you have taken out your bedding plants in the fall and then move the pansies to where you want them to bloom.

Pests and diseases: Generally trouble-free.

Uses: Flower beds and front of mixed borders, containers and informal woodland gardens.

"Viscaria" see *Lychnis*
"Wallflower, English and Siberian" see *Cheiranthus*
"Wandering Jew" see *Setcreasea*
"Wax begonia" see *Begonia*
"Wishbone flower" see *Torenia*

Xeranthemum annuum "common immortelle" ASTERACEAE
(Figure 3-11)

The common immortelle is native to Southern Europe and the Middle East and is one of the oldest known (and still one of the best) of the ever-lasting flowers. Papery petals of white, pink, purple or lilac keep their color well when dry.

Bloomtime: July to September.

Height: 24 inches (61 cm).

Light and soil: Prefers full sun and any well-drained soil.

How to grow: Although young plants are not generally available from shops, they are easily grown from seed. Sow in the garden in March. Thin to stand 18 inches (46 cm) apart and support stems with thin stakes.

Pests and diseases: Generally trouble-free.

Uses: For soft color in the mixed borders and for cut flowers, fresh and dried. To dry, cut flowers when they are fully open and hang them upside-down in bunches in a cool, airy place until dry.

Zebrina see *Setcreasea*
"Zinnia, creeping" see *Sanvitalia*

Zinnia elegans and *Zinnia haageana* "zinnia" ASTERACEAE
(Figure 4-11)

Much selecting has been done with these two species from Mexico and there is a multitude of heights and flower shapes from which to choose. Zinnias revel in hot, sunny weather and will tolerate dry soil—making them an excellent choice for a planter on a south-facing patio. Most flower colors are bright and festive and are beautifully set off by a large terra cotta pot. Leaves are triangular in outline, to 4 inches (10 cm) long, rough with prominent veins. Don't set zinnias out too early; they are best for late summer bloom, perhaps to follow schizanthus and nemesia, which fade in hot weather.

For our climate, it is better to grow the cultivars with medium or small blooms, rather than the giants. Cultivars of **Zinnia elegans** are the most widely grown. The 'Peter Pan' series, (an AAS winner), comes in mixed and separate colors of flame, orange, pink, gold, white and scarlet. Plants grow to 12–14 inches (30–36 cm) tall and bear 3-inch (7.5-cm) blooms that are fully double. The 'Ruffles' series are also AAS winners. Free-flowering, they reach 28 inches (71 cm) with 3-inch (7.5-cm) double blooms. These two series are both referred to as "cut-and-come-again" zinnias; the more flowers you cut, the more are produced.

The AAS winner, 'Border Beauty', grows to 20 inches (51 cm) with 3-inch (7.5-cm) double blooms of pink with a touch of salmon, excellent for cutting or a border. For a shorter height, try the 'Dasher' series; in separate colors of scarlet, cherry and orange, or a mix which includes yellow, pink and white, it grows to 10 inches (25 cm) with 3-inch (7.5-cm) blooms. It is especially recommended for wet, cool maritime climates.

Cultivars of **Zinnia haageana** have narrower leaves than *Zinnia elegans* and usually have two-toned flowers. Examples are 'Persian Carpet', 'Old Mexico' (an AAS winner), 'Sombrero' and 'Chippendale'. They are sometimes referred to as old-fashioned Mexican zinnias in catalogues. All reach 15 inches (38 cm), except 'Chippendale' which grows to 24 inches (61 cm).

Bloomtime: June or July to frost.

Height: 6–36 inches (15–91 cm), depending on the cultivar.

Light and soil: Prefer full sun and any well-drained soil. They will do better in a richer soil to which some organic matter has been added.

How to grow: Young plants are generally available from shops in spring, or they can be started from seed, taking advantage of cultivars not available in the trade. Sow in late March in individual 3-inch (7.5-cm) pots. Germination, at 60–70°F (15–21°C) soil temperature, takes about 5 days. Do not water with cold water or leave plants in drafts. Seedlings are susceptible to damping-off; use a fungicide drench. Set hardened-off plants out in early June, spacing them 8–12 inches (20–30 cm) apart, depending on the cultivar. Seeds can easily be sown directly in the garden in June. Seeds are large and easy to handle.

Pests and diseases: Although zinnias are generally trouble-free, a few VIRUS diseases may infect plants, causing yellow rings on the leaves. If soil is too cold and wet, seedlings may DAMP OFF or die from root ROT. In wet weather, large flowers may get GRAY MOLD and stems of very tall plants may collapse due to stem ROT.

Uses: Good for edging (blooming later than some other edging choices) and for the front of a mixed border for a festive effect. If you find zinnias too bright for your color scheme, plant them in containers on their own or in the vegetable garden for cut flowers.

QUICK REFERENCE CHART

	easy to grow	blooms June—Sept.	full sun	part shade	shade	tolerates dry soil	under 1 foot (30 cm)	1–3 feet (.3–.9 m)	over 3 feet (.9 m)	use for edging	good cut flowers	suitable for drying	good in containers	massed plantings	cottage garden style	dot plant	hanging baskets	moss baskets	winter bedding	plants readily available
Abutilon — flowering maple		•	•	•				•	•				•				•	•		
Ageratum houstonianum — flossflower	•	•	•	•			*	*		•	*		•	•					•	•
Amaranthus caudatus — love-lies-bleeding	•		•						•		•	•	•							•
Antirrhinum majus — snapdragons	•	•	•	•				•			•	•	•	•	*					•
Avena and other annual grasses	•		•					•			•	•		•						
Begonia semp.-cultorum — fibrous begonias	•	•	•	•	•	•	•			•			•	•					•	•
Begonia xtuberhybrida — tuberous begonias	•	•		•	•		*	*		•			•	•	•		•			•
Brachycome iberidifolia — Swan River daisy	•	•	•				•	•		•			•			•				•
Brassica oleracea — ornamental cabbage & kale	•		•				•						•	•				•		
Browallia — browallia	•	•	•	•	•	•	•			•			•	•	•				•	•
Calceolaria 'Sunshine' — pocketbook flower	•	•	•	•			•			•			•	•					•	•
Calendula officinalis — pot marigolds	•		•			•		•		•	•		•	•	•				•	•
Callistephus chinensis — China asters			•				*	*			•		•	•	•					
Canna xgeneralis — canna lily	•	•	•					*	*					•		•				
Catanache caerulea — cupid's dart	•	•	•	•				•		•	•	•	•							
Celosia cristata — cockscomb		•	•			•	*	*			•	•	•	•						•
Centaurea cyanus — cornflower	•		•			•		•			•				•					
Cheiranthus & Erysimum — wallflowers	•		•	•			*	*		•			•	•	•				•	•
Chrysanthemum carinatum — annual chrysanthemum	•		•					•			•			•						
Chrysanthemum frutescens — marguerite daisies	•	•	•					•			•		•	•	•					•
Chrysanthemum parthenium — feverfew	•	*	•				*	*		•	•			•	•					
Clarkia amoena — godetia	•		•					•			•				•					
Cleome hasslerana — spider flower	*		•						•					•		•				•

Short cultivars such as fuchsias are suitable as dot plants when trained as standards.

*means depending on the cultivar

| | LIGHT | | | | | HEIGHT | | | USES | | | | | | | | | | |
	easy to grow	blooms June—Sept.	full sun	part shade	shade	tolerates dry soil	under 1 foot (30 cm)	1–3 feet (.3–.9 m)	over 3 feet (.9 m)	use for edging	good cut flowers	suitable for drying	good in containers	massed plantings	cottage garden style	dot plant	hanging baskets	moss baskets	winter bedding	plants readily available
Cleretum bellidiformis Livingstone daisy	•	•	•			•	•			•			•					•		•
Coleus xhybridus coleus	•			•	•		*	*		•			•	•			•	•		•
Cordyline australis dracaena palm	•		•			•		•	•				•			•				•
Coreopsis tinctoria calliopsis	•		•					•			•		•	•	•					
Cosmos cosmos	•			•	•		*	*			•			•	•	•				•
Cuphea ignea cigar flower	•	•	•	•	•			•		•			•					•		
Dahlia hybrids dahlia	•	•	•					•		•	•		•	•						•
Dianthus barbatus sweet william	•		•					•		•	•		•	•	•				*	•
Dianthus caryophyllus carnation	•	•	•					•			•		•	•	•					•
Dianthus chinensis Indian pink	•		•					•			•		•	•	•					•
Dimorphotheca hybrids African daisy	•	•	•			•	•			•			•	•	•			•		•
Felicia amelloides blue marguerite	•	•	•					•		•	•		•	•	•		•	•		•
Fuchsia xhybrida fuchsia	•	•	*	•	•								•			•	•	•		•
Gazania xhybrida gazania	•	•	•			•	•			•			•	•				•		•
Glechoma hederacea 'Var.' trailing nepeta	•			•	•			•	•				•				•	•		•
Gomphrena globe amaranth	•	•	•				*	*		•	•	•	•	•	•					
Hedera helix English ivy	•			•	•	•		•	•				•				•	•	•	•
Helianthus annuus sunflower	•		•					*	*			*				*				
Helichrysum bracteatum strawflowers	•	•	•					*	*	*	•	•	•		•					
Heliotropium arborescens heliotrope	•	•	•	•				•		•			•	•	•					
Hypoestes phyllostachya polka dot plant	•		•	•	•			•		•			•	•				•		•
Iberis candytuft	•		•			•	*	*		•	*		•		•					
Impatiens hybrids New Guinea impatiens	•		•	•	•			•		•			•	•				•		•
Impatiens wallerana impatiens	•	•	*	•	•		•			•			•	•			•	•		•
Kochia scoparia summer cypress	•		•					•						•		•				

			LIGHT				HEIGHT			USES										
QUICK REFERENCE CHART	easy to grow	blooms June—Sept.	full sun	part shade	shade	tolerates dry soil	under 1 foot (30 cm)	1–3 feet (.3–.9 m)	over 3 feet (.9 m)	use for edging	good cut flowers	suitable for drying	good in containers	massed plantings	cottage garden style	dot plant	hanging baskets	moss baskets	winter bedding	plants readily available
Lamiastrum galeobdolon 'Var.' silver nettle vine	•		•	•	•			•	•				•				•	•		•
Lampranthus multiradiatus ice plant	•	•	•			•	•			•			•					•		•
Lantana camara lantana			•	•			*	*	*				•	•	•					
Lathyrus odoratus sweet pea	•	•	•					*	*	•			•	•	•					•
Lavatera trimestris mallow	•	•	•					*	*	•					•					
Limonium & Psylliostachys statice	•	•	•					•			•	•	•	•	•					
Lobelia erinus edging lobelia	•	•	•	•	•		•			•			•	•			•	•		•
Lobularia maritima sweet alyssum	•	•	•	•		•	•			•			•	•				•		•
Lotus berthelotii lotus vine	•		•	•			•						•				•			•
Lychnis coeli-rosea viscaria	•	•	•	•			*	*			•		•		•					
Matthiola incana stock	•		•	•				•		•	•		•	•	•					
Matthiola l. ssp. *bicornis* evening scented stock	•		•	•			•						•		•			•		
Mimulus hybrids monkey flower	•	•	•			•	•						•		•			•		
Mirabilis jalapa four-o'clocks	•		•	•			•						•		•					
Molucella laevis bells of Ireland	•	•	•				•				•	•	•		•					
Myosotis sylvatica forget-me-not	•		•	•	•		•						•	•	•				•	•
Nemesia strumosa nemesia	•		•	•	•		•			•			•	•	•			•	•	•
Nemophila menziesii baby blue eyes	•	•	•	•			•						•		•		•			•
Nicotiana alata flowering tobacco	•	•	•	•				*	*	•			•	•	•	•				•
Nierembergia hipp. var. *vio.* cupflower	•	•	•				•			•			•	•				•		
Nigella damascena love-in-a-mist	•		•				•				•	•	•		•					
Osteospermum ecklonis African daisy	•	•	•			•	•			•	•		•	•	•	•				
Papaver nudicaule Iceland poppy	•	•	•			•	*	*		•	•		•	•	•					•
Papaver rhoeas Shirley poppy	•		•			•	•			•			•	•	•					•
Pelargonium xdomesticum regal pelargonium		•		•	•		•						•							•

	LIGHT				HEIGHT				USES										
QUICK REFERENCE CHART	easy to grow	blooms June—Sept.	full sun	part shade	shade	tolerates dry soil	under 1 foot (30 cm)	1–3 feet (.3–.9 m)	over 3 feet (.9 m)	use for edging	good cut flowers	suitable for drying	good in containers	massed plantings	cottage garden style	dot plant	hanging baskets	moss baskets	winter bedding	plants readily available
Pelargonium xhortorum zonal geranium	•	•	•			•	•			•			•	•			•	•		•
Pelargonium peltatum ivy geranium	•	•		•	•		•						•				•	•		•
Petunia xhybrida petunia	•	•	•			•	•			•			•	•			•	•		•
Phlox drummondii annual phlox	•		•				*	*		•	•		•	•			•			•
Portulaca grandiflora moss rose	•	•	•			•	•			•			•	•						•
Primula xpolyantha polyanthus	•		•	•	•		•			•			•	•	•				•	•
Rudbeckia hirta black-eyed susan	•		•				•			•	•		•	•	•					•
Salpiglossis sinuata salpiglossis	•	•	•				•			•	•		•		•					
Salvia farinacea blue salvia	•	•	•				•			•	•	•	•	•	•					
Salvia splendens red salvia	•	•	•	•			*	*		•			•	•		*				•
Sanvitalia procumbens creeping zinnia	•	•	•	•		•	•			•							•	•		
Schizanthus hybrids butterfly flower	•			•	•		*	*		•			•	•	•		•	•		•
Senecio cineraria and *Chrys. ptarmiciflorum* dusty miller	•	•	•			•	•			•			•						•	•
Setcreasea et al wandering Jew	•			•	•		•						•				•	•		•
Tagetes marigolds	•	•	•			•	*	*		•	•		•	•			*		*	•
Thunbergia alata black-eyed-susan vine	•	•	•	•				•	•				•				•	•		•
Torenia fournieri wishbone flower	•			•			•			•			•				•	•		•
Tropaeolum majus nasturtium		•	•	•		•		•	•				•	•	•		•	•		•
Verbena garden verbena		•	•			•	•			•			•	•						•
Verbena trailing verbena	•	•	•	•		•	•						•	•			•	•		•
Viola pansy and violas	•	*	•	•	•		•			•			•	•	•				•	•
Xeranthemum annuum common immortelle	•	•	•				•				•	•	•	•	•					
Zinnia zinnia	•	•	•			•	*	*	*	*	•		•	•		•				•

Short cultivars such as fuchsias are suitable as dot plants when trained as standards.
*means depending on the cultivar

148

Bibliography

A Gardener's Guide to Pest Prevention and Control in the Home and Garden. Victoria: Province of BC, Ministry of Agriculture and Food, 1986.

Annuals. James Underwood Crockett and the Editors of Time-Life Books. New York: Time-Life Books, 1971.

Ball Red Book: Greenhouse Growing, 14th Edition. Edited by Dick Ball. Virginia: Reston Publishing Co., 1985.

Clark, Lewis J. *Wild Flowers of British Columbia.* Sidney: Gray's Publishing Ltd., 1973.

Crockett, James Underwood. *Crockett's Flower Garden.* Boston: Little Brown and Company, 1981.

Donahue, Roy; Schickluna, John; and Robertson, Lynn. *Soils: An Introduction to Soils and Plant Growth.* New Jersey: Prentice-Hall, Inc., 1971.

The Encyclopedia of Herbs and Herbalism. Edited by Malcolm Stuart. New York: Crescent Books, 1979.

Hortus Third. Edited by the staff of the Liberty Hyde Bailey Hortorium. New York: Macmillan Publishing Company, 1976.

149

Hunt, C. *Natural Regions of the US and Canada*. San Francisco: W.H. Freeman, 1974.

Kruckeberg, Arthur. *Gardening with Native Plants of the Pacific Northwest*. Vancouver: Douglas & McIntyre, 1982.

Lyons, C.P. *Trees, Shrubs and Flowers to Know in BC*. Toronto: J.M. Dent & Sons, 1952.

Ormsby, Margaret. *British Columbia: a History*. Vancouver: Macmillan of Canada, 1958.

Pirone, Pascal. *Diseases and Pests of Ornamental Plants, 5th Ed*. New York: John Wiley and Sons, 1978.

Pizzetti, Ippolito; and Cocker, Henry. *Flowers: A Guide for Your Garden*, Volumes I and II. New York: Harry N. Abrams Inc., 1975.

Proudley, B. and V. *Fuchsias in Color*. England: Blandford Press Ltd., 1975.

Readers Digest Encyclopaedia of Garden Plants and Flowers. Edited, designed and published by The Reader's Digest Association. London: 1985.

The Rodale Herb Book. Edited by William H. Hylton. Emmaus: Rodale Press Book Division, 1974.

Solomon, Steve. *Growing Organic Vegetables West of the Cascades*. Seattle: Pacific Search Press, 1985.

Practical Gardening Magazine. EMAP National Publications Ltd. Peterborough, PE2 0UW, England, various issues.

Commercial grower catalogue. Ball Seed Company, Missigauga, Ontario, 1987.

Commercial grower catalogue. Northrup-King Co., Minneapolis, Minnesota, 1987–88.

Commercial grower catalogue. Skagit Gardens, Mt. Vernon, Washington, 1988.

Personal communication, Robert J. Armstrong, Research Horticulturist, Longwood Gardens, Pennsylvania, USA, 1988.

Personal communication, Clive Innes, Holly Gate International, Sussex, England, 1988.

Sources

Seeds, books and accessories

Robert Bolton & Son, The Sweet Pea Specialists, Birdbrook, nr. Halstead, Essex, Great Britain, CO9 4BQ.

Butchart Gardens, Box 4010, Station A, Victoria, BC, Canada, V8X 3X4, ship to USA also.

Dominion Seed House, Georgetown, Ontario, L7G 4A2, Canada, available in Canada only.

Park Seed Company, Cokesbury Road, Greenwood, South Carolina, USA, 29647-0001, (bulbs listed also but they can not be shipped into Canada).

Stokes Seed Company
  Canadian address: 39 James St., Box 10, St. Catherines, Ontario, L2R 6R6.
  US address: P.O. Box 548, Buffalo, New York, 14240.

Thompson and Morgan Seed Catalogue, P.O. Box 1308, Jackson, New Jersey, 08527, USA, ship to Canada also.

Unwins Seeds, Histon, Cambridge, Great Britain, CB4 4LE.

Plants, bulbs and accessories (by mail order)

C.A. Cruickshank, 1015 Mount Pleasant Road, Toronto, Ontario, M4P 2M1.

Plants

Please ask the staff member in charge of buying at your favorite garden center for unusual bedding plants; they may be able to locate them for you. If not, these nurseries have some specialty items.

Chestnut Greenhouses, George van Rijn, 17974-40th Avenue, Surrey, BC, (fuchsias, geraniums and heliotrope).

Molbak's Greenhouses, 13625 NE 175th, Woodinville, Washington, (a wonderful selection of popular and unusual bedding plants and anything else imaginable for your garden).

Rainbow Garden Nursery, Pat Logie, 7091 Heather Street, Richmond, BC, (popular and unusual bedding plants including fuchsias, unusual geraniums and heliotrope).

Plant societies specializing in plants covered in this book
(write for current fees and more information)

American Begonia Society (publishes the *Begonian*), John Ingles, Jr., 8922 Conway Drive, Riverside, California, 92503, USA.

American Fuchsia Society (publishes a monthly bulletin), Hall of Flowers, Golden Gate Park, San Francisco, California, 94122, USA.

British Columbia Fuchsia and Begonia Society, Lorna Herchenson, 2402 Swinburne, North Vancouver, BC, V7H 1L2, Canada.

Canadian Geranium and Pelargonium Society, James Douglas, 3331 Dumfries Avenue, Vancouver, BC, V5C 3S4, Canada.

National Fuchsia Society, P.O. Box 4687, Downey, California, 92041, USA.

Northwest Fuchsia Society, P.O. Box 33071, Bitter Lake Station, Seattle, Washington, 98133-0071, USA.

Northwest Horticultural Society (publishes *Pacific Horticulture*), Center for Urban Horticulture, University of Washington, GF-15, Seattle, Washington, 98195, USA.

Valley Fuchsia and Geranium Club, Cliff Anderson, 2506 Cottonwood, Aldergrove, BC, V0X 1A6, Canada.

Vancouver Dahlia Society, Don Chadderton, 4545 Highland Blvd., North Vancouver, BC, V7R 3A2, Canada.

Victoria Gladiolus and Dahlia Society, Barney Marsh, 11274 Chalet Road, R.R. 1, Sydney, BC, V87 3R9, Canada.

Index

Pages given in boldface indicate encyclopedia entries.

153

About the Author

Carolyn Jones graduated from Simon Fraser University in 1974 with a bachelor's degree in biological sciences. Since then, she has enjoyed her own garden and worked in the nursery trades—in a wholesale nursery, in garden centers and as a landscape designer. She managed Massot Nurseries Garden Center, Richmond, for 2½ years and was a regular columnist for *Gardens West*. She holds a BC Pesticide Dispenser Certificate and is a member of the Vancouver Rose Society, the Alpine Garden Club of BC and the Royal Horticultural Society (Great Britain).